Lecture Notes in Computer Science 12987

More information about this subseries at https://link.springer.com/bookseries/7409

Yi Pan · Zhi-Hong Mao · Lei Luo · Jing Zeng ·
Liang-Jie Zhang (Eds.)

Artificial Intelligence and Mobile Services – AIMS 2021

10th International Conference
Held as Part of the Services Conference Federation, SCF 2021
Virtual Event, December 10–14, 2021
Proceedings

Editors
Yi Pan
Georgia State University
Atlanta, GA, USA

Lei Luo
University of Electronic Science
and Technology of China
Chengdu, China

Liang-Jie Zhang 🆔
Kingdee International Software Group
Co., Ltd.
Shenzhen, China

Zhi-Hong Mao
University of Pittsburgh
Pittsburgh, PA, USA

Jing Zeng
China Gridcom Co., Ltd.
Shenzhen, China

ISSN 0302-9743   ISSN 1611-3349 (electronic)
Lecture Notes in Computer Science
ISBN 978-3-030-96032-2   ISBN 978-3-030-96033-9 (eBook)
https://doi.org/10.1007/978-3-030-96033-9

LNCS Sublibrary: SL3 – Information Systems and Applications, incl. Internet/Web, and HCI

This Springer imprint is published by the registered company Springer Nature Switzerland AG
The registered company address is: Gewerbestrasse 11, 6330 Cham, Switzerland

Preface

The International Conference on AI and Mobile Services (AIMS 2021) aims at providing an international forum that is dedicated to exploring different aspects of AI (from technologies to approaches and algorithms) and mobile services (from business management to computing systems, algorithms, and applications) to promote technological innovations in research and development of mobile services, including, but not limited to, wireless and sensor networks, mobile and wearable computing, mobile enterprise and eCommerce, ubiquitous collaborative and social services, machine-to-machine and Internet-of-Things clouds, cyber-physical integration, and big data analytics for mobility-enabled services.

AIMS is a member of the Services Conference Federation (SCF). SCF 2021 had the following 10 collocated service-oriented sister conferences: the International Conference on Web Services (ICWS 2021), the International Conference on Cloud Computing (CLOUD 2021), the International Conference on Services Computing (SCC 2021), the International Conference on Big Data (BigData 2021), the International Conference on AI and Mobile Services (AIMS 2021), the World Congress on Services (SERVICES 2021), the International Conference on Internet of Things (ICIOT 2021), the International Conference on Cognitive Computing (ICCC 2021), the International Conference on Edge Computing (EDGE 2021), and the International Conference on Blockchain (ICBC 2021).

This volume presents the accepted papers for AIMS 2021, held as a fully virtual conference during December 10–14, 2021. The major topics of AIMS 2021 included, but were not limited to, AI modeling, AI analysis, AI and mobile applications, AI architecture, AI management, AI engineering, mobile backend as a service (MBaaS), user experience of AI, and mobile services.

We accepted nine full papers. Each paper was reviewed by three independent members of the AIMS 2021 Program Committee. We are pleased to thank the authors whose submissions and participation made this conference possible. We also want to express our thanks to the Program Committee members for their dedication in helping to organize the conference and reviewing the submissions. We look forward to your future contributions as volunteers, authors, and conference participants in the fast-growing worldwide services innovations community.

December 2021

Yi Pan
Zhi-Hong Mao
Lei Luo
Jing Zeng
Liang-Jie Zhang

Organization

AIMS 2021 General Chair

Yujiu Yang   Tsinghua University, China

AIMS 2021 Program Chairs

Yi Pan	Georgia State University, USA
Zhi-Hong Mao	University of Pittsburgh, USA
Lei Luo	University of Electronic Science and Technology of China, China
Jing Zeng	China Gridcom Co., Ltd., China

Services Conference Federation (SCF 2021)

General Chairs

Wu Chou	Essenlix Corporation, USA
Calton Pu	Georgia Tech, USA
Dimitrios Georgakopoulos	Swinburne University of Technology, Australia

Program Chairs

Liang-Jie Zhang	Kingdee International Software Group Co., Ltd., China
Ali Arsanjani	Amazon Web Services, USA

Industry Track Chairs

Awel Dico	Etihad Airways, UAE
Rajesh Subramanyan	Amazon Web Services, USA
Siva Kantamneni	Deloitte Consulting, USA

CFO

Min Luo   Georgia Tech, USA

Industry Exhibit and International Affairs Chair

Zhixiong Chen   Mercy College, USA

Operations Committee

Jing Zeng   China Gridcom Co., Ltd., China
Yishuang Ning   Tsinghua University, China
Sheng He   Tsinghua University, China

Steering Committee

Calton Pu (Co-chair)   Georgia Tech, USA
Liang-Jie Zhang (Co-chair)   Kingdee International Software Group Co., Ltd.,
                                 China

AIMS 2021 Program Committee

Yan Guo   University of International Relations, China
Ting Jin   Hainan University, China
Binyang Li   University of International Relations, China
Phuoc Hung Pham   Kent State University, USA
Xiaohui Wang   University of Science and Technology Beijing,
                                 China
Yuchao Zhang   Beijing University of Posts and
                                 Telecommunications, China

Conference Sponsor – Services Society

The Services Society (S2) is a non-profit professional organization that has been created to promote worldwide research and technical collaboration in services innovations among academia and industrial professionals. Its members are volunteers from industry and academia with common interests. S2 is registered in the USA as a "501(c) organization", which means that it is an American tax-exempt nonprofit organization. S2 collaborates with other professional organizations to sponsor or co-sponsor conferences and to promote an effective services curriculum in colleges and universities. S2 initiates and promotes a "Services University" program worldwide to bridge the gap between industrial needs and university instruction.

The services sector accounted for 79.5% of the GDP of the USA in 2016. Hong Kong has one of the world's most service-oriented economies, with the services sector accounting for more than 90% of GDP. As such, the Services Society has formed 10 Special Interest Groups (SIGs) to support technology and domain specific professional activities:

- Special Interest Group on Web Services (SIG-WS)
- Special Interest Group on Services Computing (SIG-SC)
- Special Interest Group on Services Industry (SIG-SI)
- Special Interest Group on Big Data (SIG-BD)
- Special Interest Group on Cloud Computing (SIG-CLOUD)
- Special Interest Group on Artificial Intelligence (SIG-AI)
- Special Interest Group on Edge Computing (SIG-EC)
- Special Interest Group on Cognitive Computing (SIG-CC)
- Special Interest Group on Blockchain (SIG-BC)
- Special Interest Group on Internet of Things (SIG-IOT)

About the Services Conference Federation (SCF)

As the founding member of the Services Conference Federation (SCF), the First International Conference on Web Services (ICWS) was held in June 2003 in Las Vegas, USA. A sister event, the First International Conference on Web Services - Europe 2003 (ICWS-Europe 2003), was held in Germany in October of the same year. In 2004, ICWS-Europe was changed to the European Conference on Web Services (ECOWS), which was held in Erfurt, Germany. The 19th edition in the conference series, SCF 2021, was held virtually over the Internet during December 10–14, 2021.

In the past 18 years, the ICWS community has expanded from Web engineering innovations to scientific research for the whole services industry. The service delivery platforms have expanded to mobile platforms, the Internet of Things (IoT), cloud computing, and edge computing. The services ecosystem has gradually been enabled, value added, and intelligence embedded through enabling technologies such as big data, artificial intelligence, and cognitive computing. In the coming years, transactions with multiple parties involved will be transformed by blockchain.

Based on the technology trends and best practices in the field, SCF will continue serving as the conference umbrella's code name for all services-related conferences. SCF 2021 defined the future of the New ABCDE (AI, Blockchain, Cloud, big Data, Everything is connected), which enable IoT and support the "5G for Services Era". SCF 2021 featured 10 collocated conferences all centered around the topic of "services", each focusing on exploring different themes (e.g., web-based services, cloud-based services, big data-based services, services innovation lifecycle, AI-driven ubiquitous services, blockchain-driven trust service-ecosystems, industry-specific services and applications, and emerging service-oriented technologies). The SCF 2021 members were as follows:

1. The 2021 International Conference on Web Services (ICWS 2021, http://icws.org/), which was the flagship conference for web-based services featuring web services modeling, development, publishing, discovery, composition, testing, adaptation, and delivery, as well as the latest API standards.
2. The 2021 International Conference on Cloud Computing (CLOUD 2021, http://the cloudcomputing.org/), which was the flagship conference for modeling, developing, publishing, monitoring, managing, and delivering XaaS (everything as a service) in the context of various types of cloud environments.
3. The 2021 International Conference on Big Data (BigData 2021, http://bigdataco ngress.org/), which focused on the scientific and engineering innovations of big data.
4. The 2021 International Conference on Services Computing (SCC 2021, http://the scc.org/), which was the flagship conference for the services innovation lifecycle including enterprise modeling, business consulting, solution creation, services orchestration, services optimization, services management, services marketing, and business process integration and management.

5. The 2021 International Conference on AI and Mobile Services (AIMS 2021, http://ai1000.org/), which addressed the science and technology of artificial intelligence and the development, publication, discovery, orchestration, invocation, testing, delivery, and certification of AI-enabled services and mobile applications.

6. The 2021 World Congress on Services (SERVICES 2021, http://servicescongress.org/), which put its focus on emerging service-oriented technologies and industry-specific services and solutions.

7. The 2021 International Conference on Cognitive Computing (ICCC 2021, http://thecognitivecomputing.org/), which put its focus on Sensing Intelligence (SI) as a Service (SIaaS), making a system listen, speak, see, smell, taste, understand, interact, and/or walk, in the context of scientific research and engineering solutions.

8. The 2021 International Conference on Internet of Things (ICIOT 2021, http://iciot.org/), which addressed the creation of IoT technologies and the development of IoT services.

9. The 2021 International Conference on Edge Computing (EDGE 2021, http://theedgecomputing.org/), which put its focus on the state of the art and practice of edge computing including, but not limited to, localized resource sharing, connections with the cloud, and 5G devices and applications.

10. The 2021 International Conference on Blockchain (ICBC 2021, http://blockchain1000.org/), which concentrated on blockchain-based services and enabling technologies.

Some of the highlights of SCF 2021 were as follows:

- Bigger Platform: The 10 collocated conferences (SCF 2021) got sponsorship from the Services Society, which is the world-leading not-for-profits organization (501 c(3)) dedicated to serving more than 30,000 services computing researchers and practitioners worldwide. A bigger platform means bigger opportunities for all volunteers, authors, and participants. In addition, Springer provided sponsorship for the best paper awards and other professional activities. All 10 conference proceedings of SCF 2021 will be published by Springer and indexed in the ISI Conference Proceedings Citation Index (included in the Web of Science), the Engineering Index EI (Compendex and Inspec databases), DBLP, Google Scholar, IO-Port, MathSciNet, Scopus, and ZBlMath.

- Brighter Future: While celebrating the 2021 version of ICWS, SCF 2021 highlighted the Fourth International Conference on Blockchain (ICBC 2021) to build the fundamental infrastructure for enabling secure and trusted services ecosystems. It will also lead our community members to create their own brighter future.

- Better Model: SCF 2021 continued to leverage the invented Conference Blockchain Model (CBM) to innovate the organizing practices for all 10 collocated conferences.

Contents

Contents

Research Track

A Combination of Resampling Method and Machine Learning for Text Classification on Imbalanced Data

Haijun Feng[✉], Tangren Dan, Weiming Wang, Rongzhi Gui, Junyao Liu, and Yi Li

Shenzhen Institute of Information Technology, Shenzhen 518172, China
fenghj@sziit.edu.cn

Abstract. Imbalanced data will affect the accuracy of text classification, in order to solve this issue, 11 different algorithms are used to resampling the dataset. Results show that, 5 different oversampling method and SmoteTomek method can rebalance the dataset effectively, which can improve the recognition rate of models on the minority class obviously, while undersampling methods decrease the overall accuracy of models on imbalanced dataset. Meanwhile, 7 different machine learning algorithms are used to train the model with datasets resampled by SmoteTomek algorithm, after combination, Naive Bayes and Logistic Regression algorithms performs best, they can improve the predictive ability of models on the minority class significantly without decreasing the overall accuracy of models. So in handling multi-class imbalanced text classification, Naive Bayes or Logistic Regression combined with SmoteTomek resampling method should be a preference.

Keywords: Imbalanced data · Machine learning · Undersampling · Oversampling · Text classification · Naive Bayes

1 Introduction

Text classification plays an important a role in nature language processing, it is also a very important application of machine learning. Classifying text automatically by machine can save manpower and time, it is widely applied in different areas such as biomedical science, finance and information technology.

In order to train a classifier which is accurate, high quality dataset is needed. But in reality, datasets have different problems which can affect training a model. One of these problems is that the dataset is imbalanced, which means the major class have lots of samples while the minor class has only a few samples. Classifier trained by this dataset will prone to the major class and has a very poor prediction in the minor class [1–3].

Solutions to imbalanced issues are mainly researched in two directions. One direction is adjusting the algorithms to improve the prediction ability of models, such as cost-sensitive learning, ensemble method. Bagging [4] and Boosting [5] are two common ensemble methods which are used to train models with imbalanced dataset.

Y. Pan et al. (Eds.): AIMS 2021, LNCS 12987, pp. 3–17, 2022.
https://doi.org/10.1007/978-3-030-96033-9_1

The other direction is to introduce resampling technique to balance the dataset, including oversampling and under-sampling methods. Popular over-sampling algorithm includes Smote [6], BorderlineSmote [7], ADASYN [8], RandomOverSampler and so on. The mail goal of these methods is to increase the samples of the minority classes by different ways, while under-sampling methods will drop samples from the majority classes to balance the dataset. Common under-sampling methods include ENN [9], TomekLinks [10], RandomUnderSampler, OneSidedSelection [11], InstanceHardnessThreshold [12]. Both over-sampling and under-sampling method can solve imbalanced issue to a certain extent, but new problems can be introduced, lots of replicas in over-sampling methods can cause over-fitting in model training. Dropping feature data in under-sampling method will decrease the overall accuracy of models. So in order to solve these problems, we need to combine over-sampling and under-sampling method together to train models. SmoteTomek [13] and SmoteENN [14] are popular combining methods. Douzas [15] proposes an oversampling method based on k-means clustering and SMOTE, this method avoids the generation of noise when generating new samples and it overcomes imbalances between and within classes effectively. Lin [16] introduces two undersampling strategies with clustering technique when preprocessing data, In the first strategy, cluster centers represent the majority class, in the second strategy, the nearest neighbors of the cluster centers is used. They find the second strategy is better. Zhu [17] proposes k-nearest neighbors (k-NN)-based synthetic minority oversampling algorithm(termed SMOM) to handle imbalanced issues, SMOM avoids over generalization in yielding the synthetic instances. This method gets effectiveness on lots of real-world datasets. Li [18] proposes a swarm fusion method which uses stochastic swarm heuristics to optimize the mixtures cooperatively. This fusion strategy can find the optimal mix closely with better accuracy and reliability. What's more, the computational speed is higher.

In this paper, researches are carried out on the data level, In order to find the best method to handle the imbalanced issue, 11 different algorithms are used to resample the dataset, and then we train the model with different resampled datasets and analyze the accuracy of classifiers. Meanwhile, 7 different machine learning methods (Decision Tree [19], KNN, Logistic Regression [20], Naive Bayes [21], Neural Network [22], Random Forest [19], SVM) are combined with resampling algorithms to train the model.

The rest of the paper is organized as follows: Sect. 2 introduces our methods and experimental details. Section 3 introduces our experiment, discusses and compares the effect of different combined methods. Section 4 gives the conclusions and recommends the best combined method in dealing with imbalanced datasets.

2 Methods and Experiments

2.1 Methods

The workflow of method is showed in Fig. 1, in this work, we first clean the dataset from the corpus, then we segment the Chinese words and remove stop words, after the preprocessing, we transform the Chinese words into bags of words and then TF-IDF [21]. Next, 11 different algorithms are used to resample the dataset respectively, in order to get a relatively balanced dataset. Afterwards, Naïve Bayes method [21] is carried out to train the model with different resampled datasets, then we evaluate the model and analyze the effect of different resampling algorithms. Meanwhile, 7 different machine learning methods are used to train the model respectively with the dataset resampled by SmoteTomek [13] algorithm; we also evaluate the model and analyze the influence of resampling on different machine learning methods.

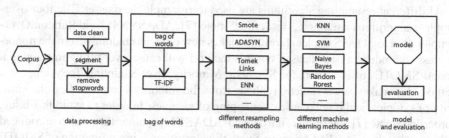

data processing   bag of words   different resampling   different machine   model
                                      methods   learning methods   and evaluation

Fig. 1. Workflow of the method

2.2 Experimental Details

Python language and Jupyter notebook are used to carry out the experiment, SciKit-learn [23] and imbalanced-learn [24] libraries are also introduced. All experiments are running on Baidu AI studio.

The dataset in this paper is collected from customer reviews of retailers online. Five categories are picked to train the model, including mobile phones, fruits, water heaters, clothes and computers. The total dataset has 26856 samples, in the experiment, 80% of the dataset is picked out randomly to work as the training set, and the rest 20% part is used as the test set. The profile of dataset is showed in Table 1. The major class fruits has 9992 instants and the minor class water heaters have only 573 instants, the ratio is 17.4:1, which is an imbalanced dataset.

Table 1. Dataset profile of 5 shopping categories

	Items	Number
1	Fruits	9992
2	Clothes	9985
3	Computers	3983
4	Mobile phones	2323
5	Water heaters	573

In the experiment, jieba tool is used to segment the Chinese words and stop words is removed according to the Chinese stop words list. Then the words are transformed into Term Frequency-Inverse Document Frequency (TF-IDF [21]), high frequency words which occur in 80% of samples are removed; low frequency words which occur less than 3 times are also removed. After the preprocessing, the total number of feature words is 8934.

11 different resampling algorithms are used to resample the dataset. The four over-sampling algorithms are Smote, BorderlineSmote [7], ADASYN [8] and RandomOver-Sampler. RandomOverSampler algorithm makes new replicas randomly from the minor-ity class to produce a new dataset, but this method will cause over fitting in training a model. SMOTE [6] is a short for Synthetic Minority Over-Sampling Technique, this method also makes new synthetic replicas from the minority class based on the simi-larity of samples, and it will cause overlapping of samples. In order to avoid this issue, BorderlineSmote [7] algorithm is introduced. ADASYN [8] algorithm is also introduced in this work, which is called Adaptive Synthetic algorithm, it is a promotion of SMOTE [6] method.

Five under sampling algorithms (ENN [9], TomekLinks [10], RandomUnderSam-pler, OneSidedSelection [11] and InstanceHardnessThreshold [12]) are also carried out to resample the dataset. RandomUnderSampler method drops samples randomly from the majority class; this method will cause the loss of feature data. TomekLinks [10] is an under-sampling method by removing Tomek's links. ENN [9] stands for Edited Nearest Neighbours, this method will under sample the dataset by removing samples near the decision boundary. In OneSidedSelection [11] method, noises and boundary data from the majority classes are removed to build a new balanced dataset. Instance-HardnessThreshold [12] method will clean the dataset by removing samples whose probability of occurrence is below the threshold.

Two combined methods (SmoteTomek [13] and SmoteENN [14]) are also introduced in this work. SmoteTomek [13] method is a combination of Smote and TomekLinks, it use Smote method to generate new samples from the minority classes and Tomek's links are removed to build a new dataset. SmoteENN [14] method is a combination of Smote and ENN, it also use Smote method to extend the minority class, and then samples next to the boundary are cleaned by ENN method.

After resampling by different algorithms, we get the new training set, which is illustrated in Table 2. From this table, we can see, the 4 oversampling algorithms and SmoteTomek can balance the dataset well. While among the undersampling algorithm, only RandomUnderSampler algorithms can balance the dataset, but this method drops too many instants.

Table 2. Training set profile of 5 shopping categories after resampling

	Fruits	Clothes	Computers	Mobile phones	Water heaters
Original training set	7978	8026	3187	1835	458
Smote	8026	8026	8026	8026	8026
BorderlineSmote	8026	8026	8026	8026	8026
ADASYN	7978	8026	9419	8622	7970
RandomOverSampler	8026	8026	8026	8026	8026
ENN	589	2378	1	199	458
TomekLinks	7841	7871	3169	1809	458
RandomUnderSampler	458	458	458	458	458
OneSidedSelection	7840	7867	3169	1809	458
InstanceHardnessThreshold	768	967	469	458	458
SmoteTomek	7948	7946	8025	8022	8023
SmoteENN	394	1486	5202	7673	7713

3   Results and Discussions

3.1   Evaluation Metrics

The classification in this experiment belongs to a multi-class classification. In this situation, precision, recall, f1score, overall accuracy (acc) and confusion matrix are picked together to evaluate the classifier. The metrics are defined as below respectively:

$$\mathrm{Pr}ecision = \frac{TP}{TP + FP} \tag{1}$$

$$\mathrm{Re}call = \frac{TP}{TP + FN} \tag{2}$$

$$f1score = 2 * \frac{\mathrm{Pr}ecision * \mathrm{Re}call}{\mathrm{Pr}ecision + \mathrm{Re}call} \tag{3}$$

$$acc = \frac{TP + TN}{TP + TN + FP + FN} \tag{4}$$

In the formulas, TP stands for true positives, TN for true negatives, FP for false positives and FN for false negatives. Recall is a nice metric in evaluating a multi-class text classification problem, which shows the prediction of true positives by the classifier.

3.2   Results of Different Resampling Methods

For the imbalanced dataset, 11 different algorithms are used to resample the dataset in this experiment, then we use Naive Bayes [21] method to train the model, the result is showed in Table 3. From this table, we can get that, for the original dataset, the recall of class "water heaters" is 0.043, which means the classifier has a very bad prediction on the minor class. For class "mobile phones", the recall is 0.863, this is also not a very good prediction compared to other classes. The reason lies in the dataset, the number of samples of water heaters and mobile phones is 573 and 2323 respectively, which is much smaller than other classes. The imbalanced issue causes the bad prediction of model on minor classes.

After resampled by 4 different oversampling methods(Smote [6], BorderlineSmote [7], ADASYN [8], RandomOverSampler) the prediction of the model on minor class "mobile phones" and "water heaters" is obviously improved. The recall of "mobile phones" and "water heaters" is improved to above 0.9 and 0.8 respectively; the overall accuracy is improved to 0.932 from 0.928, which means the 4 different resampling algorithms can balance the dataset and solve the imbalanced issue. F1score shows the same results. These oversampling methods can improve the prediction ability of model on minor classes even if they have only a few samples.

From Table 3, we can get none of the five undersampling algorithms (ENN [9], TomekLinks [10], RandomUnderSampler, OneSidedSelection [11], InstanceHardnessThreshold [12]) can handle imbalanced issues well. After resampling by TomekLinks and OneSidedSelection algorithms, the precision of the classifier is almost the same as that trained by original dataset. The two methods cannot improve the prediction ability of model on minor classes. The other three algorithm can improve the prediction ability of model on minor classes to a contain extent, but these methods drop too many samples, which descend the overall accuracy of the model. After all, in handling imbalanced issues, undersampling algorithms cannot get a perfect effect.

As the combination method, SmoteTomek [13] algorithm can improve the prediction ability of model on minor classes effectively, it can also improve the overall accuracy of the model; SmoteENN [14] algorithm can also improve the precision of model on minor classes, but it reduces the prediction ability of model on other classes, descending the overall accuracy of classifier to 0.5, which is not a very effective method in this situation.

Table 3. Metrics of model trained with datasets resampled by different algorithms

Class	Method	Recall	Precision	F1score	Acc
Mobile phones	Original training set	0.863	0.988	0.921	0.928
	Smote	0.943	0.947	0.945	0.933
	BorderlineSmote	0.953	0.910	0.931	0.932
	ADASYN	0.939	0.952	0.945	0.932
	RandomOverSampler	0.943	0.948	0.946	0.933
	ENN	0.398	0.946	0.560	0.625
	TomekLinks	0.865	0.988	0.922	0.928

(continued)

Table 3. (*continued*)

Class	Method	Recall	Precision	F1score	Acc
	RandomUnderSampler	0.932	0.889	0.910	0.894
	OneSidedSelection	0.865	0.988	0.922	0.928
	InstanceHardnessThreshold	0.893	0.881	0.887	0.893
	SmoteTomek	0.941	0.948	0.944	0.932
	SmoteENN	0.961	0.459	0.621	0.5
Fruits	Original training set	0.966	0.918	0.941	0.928
	Smote	0.950	0.952	0.951	0.933
	BorderlineSmote	0.952	0.947	0.949	0.932
	ADASYN	0.949	0.956	0.952	0.932
	RandomOverSampler	0.949	0.955	0.952	0.933
	ENN	0.575	0.985	0.726	0.625
	TomekLinks	0.966	0.919	0.942	0.928
	RandomUnderSampler	0.907	0.938	0.922	0.894
	OneSidedSelection	0.966	0.919	0.942	0.928
	InstanceHardnessThreshold	0.914	0.924	0.919	0.893
	SmoteTomek	0.949	0.951	0.950	0.932
	SmoteENN	0.185	1	0.312	0.5
Water heaters	Original training set	0.043	1	0.083	0.928
	Smote	0.826	0.450	0.583	0.933
	BorderlineSmote	0.852	0.492	0.624	0.932
	ADASYN	0.826	0.444	0.578	0.932
	RandomOverSampler	0.843	0.429	0.569	0.933
	ENN	0.435	0.309	0.361	0.625
	TomekLinks	0.043	1	0.083	0.928
	RandomUnderSampler	0.887	0.314	0.464	0.894
	OneSidedSelection	0.043	1	0.083	0.928
	InstanceHardnessThreshold	0.757	0.431	0.549	0.893
	SmoteTomek	0.826	0.448	0.581	0.932
	SmoteENN	0.957	0.064	0.120	0.5
Clothes	Original training set	0.949	0.923	0.936	0.928
	Smote	0.912	0.962	0.936	0.933
	BorderlineSmote	0.916	0.959	0.937	0.932
	ADASYN	0.908	0.963	0.935	0.932
	RandomOverSampler	0.911	0.962	0.936	0.933
	ENN	0.999	0.511	0.676	0.625
	TomekLinks	0.948	0.923	0.936	0.928
	RandomUnderSampler	0.857	0.947	0.900	0.894
	OneSidedSelection	0.948	0.923	0.936	0.928
	InstanceHardnessThreshold	0.912	0.889	0.900	0.893

(*continued*)

Table 3. (*continued*)

Class	Method	Recall	Precision	F1score	Acc
	SmoteTomek	0.911	0.962	0.936	0.932
	SmoteENN	0.510	0.930	0.659	0.5
Computers	Original training set	0.946	0.930	0.938	0.928
	Smote	0.954	0.941	0.947	0.933
	BorderlineSmote	0.922	0.956	0.939	0.932
	ADASYN	0.961	0.921	0.940	0.932
	RandomOverSampler	0.956	0.948	0.952	0.933
	ENN	0	0	0	0.625
	TomekLinks	0.946	0.930	0.938	0.928
	RandomUnderSampler	0.932	0.912	0.922	0.894
	OneSidedSelection	0.946	0.930	0.938	0.928
	InstanceHardnessThreshold	0.812	0.961	0.880	0.893
	SmoteTomek	0.954	0.936	0.945	0.932
	SmoteENN	0.925	0.621	0.743	0.5

Figure 2 shows recall of classifiers trained by different resampling method, the four different oversampling methods and combination method SmoteTomek can improve the recognition rate of classifiers on minor classes (mobile phones and water heaters). The recall of minor class water heaters can be improved to above 0.8 and the recall of other classes are all above 0.9. While for the five undersampling algorithms and combination method SmoteENN, the recall of models fluctuates a lot after dataset resampled. For some classes, the recall drops below 0.2, which decreasing the overall accuracy of the model. The main reason lies in lots of feature data lost in undersampling, which leads to an insufficient learning in model training.

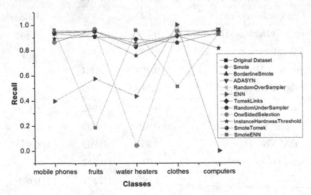

Fig. 2. Recall of classifiers trained by different resampling method

We can get further understanding of the model by confusion matrix. Figure 3(a) and (b) is the confusion matrix of model trained by original dataset and resampled dataset with SmoteTomek algorithm respectively. From Fig. 3(a), the recall of model on minor class water heaters is very small; the reason is lots of water heaters are predicted as clothes and other classes. While after resampled by SmoteTomek algorithm, the recognition rate of the model on class water heaters is improving obviously, as showed in Fig. 3(b), most water heaters can be distinguished. Meanwhile, the other classes can also be predicted correctly. From the above discussion, we can get that SmoteTomek algorithm can overcome the imbalanced issue of dataset and improve the recognition rate of model on each class.

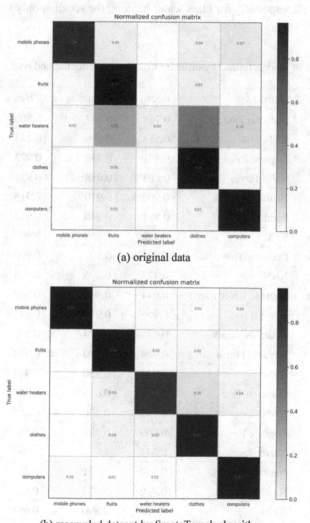

(a) original data

(b) resampled dataset by SmoteTomek algorithm

Fig. 3. Confusion matrix of model

3.3 Result Discussions of Different Machine Learning Algorithm

In order to better combine resampling algorithms and machine learning methods, we also use different machine learning method to train the model with dataset resampled by SmoteTomek [13]. 7 common machine learning methods (Decision Tree [19], KNN, Logistic Regression [20], Naive Bayes [21], Neural Network [22], Random Forest [19], SVM) are used respectively. Then we compare the effect of each model and discuss the difference.

Recall of different models trained by original dataset is showed in Table 4. The prediction ability of model trained by KNN method is poor on all classes in this situation, for the other 6 methods, models all prone to predict major classes and cannot recognize minor classes well, especially for class water heaters, the recall is only 0.043 by Naive Bayes [21].

Table 4. Metrics of models trained by different machine learning method with original dataset

Class	Method	Recall	Precision	F1score	Acc
Mobile phones	Decision Tree	0.768	0.847	0.806	0.879
	KNN	0.533	0.159	0.245	0.419
	Logistic Regression	0.881	0.973	0.925	0.931
	Naive Bayes	0.863	0.988	0.921	0.928
	Neural Network	0.900	0.930	0.915	0.918
	Random Forest	0.891	0.940	0.915	0.922
	SVM	0.912	0.959	0.935	0.940
Fruits	Decision Tree	0.905	0.907	0.906	0.879
	KNN	0.474	0.495	0.484	0.419
	Logistic Regression	0.944	0.940	0.942	0.931
	Naive Bayes	0.966	0.918	0.941	0.928
	Neural Network	0.936	0.924	0.930	0.918
	Random Forest	0.929	0.940	0.934	0.922
	SVM	0.944	0.950	0.947	0.940
Water heaters	Decision Tree	0.539	0.633	0.582	0.879
	KNN	0.139	0.390	0.205	0.419
	Logistic Regression	0.400	0.939	0.561	0.931
	Naive Bayes	0.043	1	0.083	0.928
	Neural Network	0.557	0.621	0.587	0.918
	Random Forest	0.496	0.826	0.620	0.922
	SVM	0.565	0.890	0.691	0.940
Clothes	Decision Tree	0.915	0.880	0.897	0.879

(continued)

Table 4. (*continued*)

Class	Method	Recall	Precision	F1score	Acc
	KNN	0.520	0.577	0.547	0.419
	Logistic Regression	0.959	0.905	0.931	0.931
	Naive Bayes	0.949	0.923	0.936	0.928
	Neural Network	0.926	0.914	0.920	0.918
	Random Forest	0.954	0.889	0.920	0.922
	SVM	0.960	0.920	0.940	0.940
Computers	Decision Tree	0.842	0.851	0.846	0.879
	KNN	0.001	1	0.003	0.419
	Logistic Regression	0.935	0.953	0.944	0.931
	Naive Bayes	0.946	0.930	0.938	0.928
	Neural Network	0.913	0.940	0.927	0.918
	Random Forest	0.908	0.968	0.937	0.922
	SVM	0.947	0.956	0.951	0.940

SmoteTomek [13] algorithm is used to resample the dataset, then 7 different machine learning method are used to train the model again, the result is showed in Table 5, after resampling, recall of most models on minor classes is improved, especially for Naive Bayes [21] method, recall of minor class water heaters is improved from 0.043 to 0.826; for Logistic Regression method, the recall of minor class is improved from 0.4 to 0.809, which is also a big progress. Obviously, SmoteTomek algorithm can increase the prediction ability of models on minor classes.

Table 5. Metrics of models trained by different machine learning method with datasets resampled by SmoteTomek algorithm

Class	Method	Recall	Precision	F1score	Acc
Mobile phones	Decision tree	0.830	0.697	0.758	0.851
	KNN	0.961	0.174	0.295	0.237
	Logistic regression	0.955	0.790	0.865	0.917
	Naive Bayes	0.941	0.948	0.944	0.932
	Neural Network	0.934	0.867	0.899	0.919
	Random forest	0.930	0.783	0.850	0.908
	SVM	0.947	0.854	0.898	0.927
Fruits	Decision Tree	0.876	0.907	0.891	0.851

(*continued*)

Table 5. (*continued*)

Class	Method	Recall	Precision	F1score	Acc
	KNN	0.094	0.855	0.169	0.237
	Logistic regression	0.928	0.969	0.948	0.917
	Naive Bayes	0.949	0.951	0.950	0.932
	Neural network	0.936	0.943	0.939	0.919
	Random Forest	0.921	0.942	0.931	0.908
	SVM	0.937	0.965	0.951	0.927
Water heaters	Decision tree	0.600	0.383	0.468	0.851
	KNN	0.843	0.051	0.096	0.237
	Logistic regression	0.809	0.441	0.571	0.917
	Naive Bayes	0.826	0.448	0.581	0.932
	Neural network	0.704	0.488	0.577	0.919
	Random forest	0.661	0.524	0.585	0.908
	SVM	0.730	0.483	0.581	0.927
Clothes	Decision tree	0.869	0.884	0.876	0.851
	KNN	0.240	0.955	0.384	0.237
	Logistic regression	0.904	0.945	0.924	0.917
	Naive Bayes	0.911	0.962	0.936	0.932
	Neural network	0.915	0.941	0.928	0.919
	Random forest	0.926	0.914	0.920	0.908
	SVM	0.920	0.942	0.931	0.927
Computers	Decision tree	0.796	0.857	0.826	0.851
	KNN	0.057	0.865	0.106	0.237
	Logistic regression	0.917	0.948	0.932	0.917
	Naive Bayes	0.954	0.936	0.945	0.932
	Neural network	0.910	0.935	0.922	0.919
	Random forest	0.853	0.980	0.912	0.908
	SVM	0.933	0.942	0.938	0.927

From Fig. 4, we can find that the recognition rate of model on minor class is improved intuitively after dataset resampled by SmoteTomek [13]. Naive Bayes [21] method get the best promotion, followed by Logistic Regression [20] method. We think, the reason lies in the prior probability of Naive Bayes [21] method, which is sensitive to the number variance of samples.

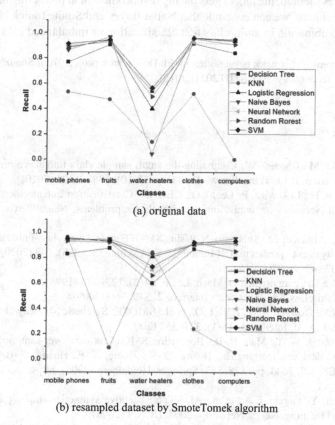

(a) original data

(b) resampled dataset by SmoteTomek algorithm

Fig. 4. Recall of models trained by different machine learning methods

4 Conclusions

In order to solve the imbalanced issue of text classification, 11 different algorithms are used to resampling the dataset, including 4 oversampling methods, 5 undersampling methods and 2 combination methods. The 4 oversampling algorithm can solve the imbalanced issue effectively and improve the recognition rate of model on minor classes, without reducing the overall accuracy. The 5 undersampling algorithm can improve the recall of minor class to a certain extent, but they decrease the prediction ability of model on major classes because of discarding of feature samples. Among the 2 combination methods, only SmoteTomek algorithm can improve the prediction ability of models on both major and minor classes. After all, in handling the multi-class text classification of imbalanced data, BorderlineSmote and SmoteTomek algorithms can be a preference in resampling datasets. Meanwhile, 7 different machine learning methods are also used to train the model with datasets resampled by SmoteTomek algorithm. All machine learning methods get a more precise model with dataset resampled by SmoteTomek. Especially for Naive Bayes method, the model gets the biggest promotion in predicting minor class. From the experiment, we can conclude that Naïve Bayes and SmoteTomek algorithm is very useful combination in multi-class text classification of imbalanced data.

Acknowledgement. This work is supported by Ph.D. research project from Shenzhen Institute of Information Technology (NO: SZIIT2021KJ012).

References

1. Wasikowski, M., Chen, X.W.: Combating the small sample class imbalance problem using feature selection. IEEE Trans. Knowl. Data Eng. **22**(10), 1388–1400 (2010)
2. Suh, S., Lee, H., Lukowicz, P., Lee, Y.O.: CEGAN: Classification Enhancement Generative Adversarial Networks for unraveling data imbalance problems. Neural Netw. **133**, 69–86 (2021)
3. Kumari, C., Abulaish, M., Subbarao, N.: Using SMOTE to deal with class-imbalance problem in bioactivity data to predict mTOR Inhibitors. SN Comput. Sci. **1**(3), 1–7 (2020). https://doi.org/10.1007/s42979-020-00156-5
4. Breiman, L.: Bagging predictors. Mach. Learn. **24**(2), 123–140 (1996)
5. Zhu, J.: Multi-class AdaBoost. Stats Interface **2**, 349–360 (2009)
6. Chawla, N.V., Bowyer, K.W., Hall, L.O., et al.: SMOTE: Synthetic Minority Over-sampling Technique. J. Artif. Intell. Res. **16**(1), 321–357 (2002)
7. Han, H., Wang, W.-Y., Mao, B.-H.: Borderline-SMOTE: a new over-sampling method in imbalanced data sets learning. In: Huang, D.-S., Zhang, X.-P., Huang, G.-B. (eds.) ICIC 2005. LNCS, vol. 3644, pp. 878–887. Springer, Heidelberg (2005). https://doi.org/10.1007/11538059_91
8. He, H., Bai, Y., Garcia, E.A., et al.: ADASYN: adaptive synthetic sampling approach for imbalanced learning. Neural Networks, 2008. IJCNN (2008)
9. Wilson, D.L.: Asymptotic properties of nearest neighbor rules using edited data. IEEE Trans. Syst. Man Cybern. **2**(3), 408–421 (2007)
10. Tomek, I.: Two modifications of CNN. IEEE Trans. Syst. Man Cybern. SMC-6(11), 769–772 (1976)
11. Kubat, M., Matwin, S.: Addressing the curse of imbalanced training sets: one-sided selection. ICML **97**, 179–186 (1997)
12. Smith, M.R., Martinez, T., Giraud-Carrier, C.: An instance level analysis of data complexity. Mach. Learn. **95**(2), 225–256 (2014)
13. Batista, G.E., Bazzan, A.L.C., Monard, M.C.: Balancing training data for automated annotation of keywords: a case study. II Brazilian Workshop on Bioinformatics, pp. 10–18 (2008)
14. Batista, G.E.A.P., Prati, R.C., Monard, M.C.: A study of the behavior of several methods for balancing machine learning training data. ACM SIGKDD Explor. Newsl **6**(1), 20–29 (2004)
15. Georgios, D., Fernando, B., Felix, L.: Improving imbalanced learning through a heuristic oversampling method based on k-means and SMOTE. Inf. Sci. **465**, 1–20 (2018)

16. Lin, W.C., Tsai, C.F., Hu, Y.H., et al.: Clustering-based undersampling in class-imbalanced data. Inf. Sci. **409**, 17–26 (2017)
17. Zhu, T., Lin, Y., Liu, Y.: Synthetic minority oversampling technique for multiclass imbalance problems. Pattern Recogn. **72**, 327–340 (2017)
18. Li, J., Fong, S., Wong, R.K., et al.: Adaptive multi-objective swarm fusion for imbalanced data classification. Inf. Fusion **39**, 1–24 (2018)
19. Breiman, L.: Random forests. Mach. Learn. **45**(1), 5–32 (2001)
20. Yu, H.F., Huang, F.L., Lin, C.J.: Dual coordinate descent methods for logistic regression and maximum entropy models. Mach. Learn. **85**(1–2), 41–75 (2011)
21. Manning, C.D., Raghavan, P., Schütze, H.: Introduction to Information Retrieval. Cambridge University Press, Cambridge (2008)
22. Glorot, X., Bengio, Y.: Understanding the difficulty of training deep feedforward neural networks. J. Mach. Learn. Res. **9**, 249–256 (2010)
23. Swami, A., Jain, R.: Scikit-learn: machine learning in python. J. Mach. Learn. Res. **12**(10), 2825–2830 (2011)
24. Lemaitre, G., Nogueira, F., Aridas, C.K.: Imbalanced-learn: a python toolbox to tackle the curse of imbalanced datasets in machine learning. J. Mach. Learn. Res. **18**(17), 1–5 (2017)

A Privacy Knowledge Transfer Method for Clinical Concept Extraction

Xuan Luo, Yiping Yin, Yice Zhang, and Ruifeng Xu[✉]

Harbin Institute of Technology (Shenzhen), Shenzhen, China
xuruifeng@hit.edu.cn

Abstract. Recent works have revealed that there is a training data leakage hazard in deep learning models, which is catastrophic for tasks like clinical concept extraction with high privacy requirements. Therefore, to alleviate privacy leakage during the model release phase, this paper propose a knowledge distillation based privacy protection method. The proposed method follows the teacher-student framework and utilizes a novel distillation method for sequence labeling so that the final model is trained without direct contact with sensitive source data. This paper mainly focuses on the scenario where the training data is multi-source and heterogeneous, and correspondingly proposes a re-normalization operation and weight adjustment strategy for knowledge aggregation. Experiment results on the public dataset show that the proposed privacy protection method could achieve comparable performance to the fully supervised method, demonstrating the effectiveness of the proposed method.

Keywords: Clinical concept extraction · Privacy protection · Knowledge distillation

1 Introduction

Clinical Concept Extraction (CCE) aims to extract predefined medical concepts from unstructured text, and is a primary step in the analysis of Electronic Health Records [15]. Deep learning based CCE research has increased rapidly in recent years [6]. In these works, CCE is usually formalized as a sequence labeling task [11]. First, a language encoder (e.g. BERT [3]) is employed to produce contextual representation, and then Conditional Random Field [8] (CRF) is utilized for the inference of the label sequence. Since deep learning methods do not require complicated feature engineering and have promising performance, they have become the mainstream approaches in CCE.

However, existing works [1,5,14,16] show that it is feasible to infer the training data from deep learning models, but these data in CCE are often sensitive and private. Hence, the main peril is the privacy leakage of CCE methods based on deep learning. Besides, a complete, high-performance deep model often requires huge amount of training data while clinical data are often scattered in different

© Springer Nature Switzerland AG 2022
Y. Pan et al. (Eds.): AIMS 2021, LNCS 12987, pp. 18–28, 2022.
https://doi.org/10.1007/978-3-030-96033-9_2

organizations and hardly shared for the sake of privacy and intellectual property protection.

In order to solve the above problems, we follow the idea of Papernot et al. [12]. First, we train multiple teacher models on sensitive data from different sources, and then transfer the knowledge from multiple teacher models to a single student model through an unlabeled, non-sensitive transfer set. With this strategy, the training of the student model does not directly depend on the sensitive training data, so the privacy of the sensitive data is protected to a large extent. In order to achieve more efficient knowledge transfer between teachers and the student, we replace the original voting strategy with Knowledge Distillation [7].

In practice, since the data from different institutions are often independently labeled, the corresponding label sets are not identical. To obtain a complete student model, these label sets are supposed to be merged, which makes the teacher models and the student model heterogeneous. In order to transfer heterogeneous knowledge in CCE, we apply re-normalization operation to achieve the alignment among heterogeneous label sets, and introduce a weight adjusting strategy to reduce the category bias of teacher models.

Experiment results on public dataset attest the effectiveness of our method. The student model reaches a comparable performance to the teacher model, with only 0.92% lower in F1 value than that of the fully supervised method.

2   Related Work

Knowledge Distillation. Knowledge distillation (KD) is widely used for model compression. KD transfers knowledge from a large model (also called the teacher model) to a smaller model (the student model) without loss of validity. The teacher-student framework guarantees that the student can be trained with data different from the teacher's, so that the training data in the teacher model is invisible for the student.

Ross et al. [13] demonstrated that the robustness of teacher's output is resilient to the perturbation of adversarial samples. Lopes et al. [10] proposed to distill without training data. It generate the training data for the student from the active layer of the teacher. Papernot et al. [12] proposed to train several teachers with private data and utilize the distilled knowledge to supervise the student trained on public data. It aggregated the privacy knowledge by voting. However, in practice, the label sets of different teachers may be differ and it does not take the data bias into consideration. So we propose a multi-teacher distillation framework to solve the problems.

Pre-trained Language Model. The advent of pre-trained language models (PLMs) implys a new era of natural language processing. Considerable work has shown that PLMs, trained on the large corpus, can learn universal language representations, which are beneficial for downstream tasks and can avoid training a new model from scratch. The second-generation PLMs, such as BERT [3], focus on learning contextual word embeddings. PLMs usually provide a better model initialization, leading to a better generalization performance. So we utilize the BERT combined with CRF [8] layer for sequence labeling task.

3   Preliminaries

3.1   Clinical Concept Extraction and Sequence Labeling

Given a text $\mathbf{x} = [x_1, x_2, ..., x_T]$ of length T, the goal of clinical concept extraction (CCE) is to obtain the concept set $C = \{(c_1, l_1), (c_2, l_2), ..., (c_{|C|}, l_{|C|})\}$, where $c_i = [w_{i1}, w_{i2}, ..., w_{ik}]$ is a text span of $\mathbf{x}$, and l_i is the concept type.

The CCE task is often formalized as a sequence labeling [11] task. Under this formalization, the concept set C is transformed into a label sequence $\mathbf{y} = [y_1, y_2, \cdots, y_T]$. The label of each word is assigned according to its position within the concept and the corresponding concept type. More specifically, the label space $V = \{B - t_1, \cdots, B - t_{|T|}, I - t_1, \cdots, I - l_{|T|}, O\}$, where $B - t_i$ indicates that the corresponding word is at the beginning of a concept of type t_i; $I - t_i$ indicates that this word is in the middle or at the end of a concept of type t_i; O indicates that this word is not included in any concept.

The sequence labeling task can be solved directly through a linear classifier. Assuming that $H = [\mathbf{h}_1, \mathbf{h}_2, \cdots, \mathbf{h}_T]$ is the contextual representation of text $\mathbf{x}$ produced by a language encoder, then the conditional probability can be calculated by the following formula:

$$f(x_t, y) = W_y^\top \mathbf{h}_t, \tag{1}$$

$$p(y_t | x_t) = \frac{\exp f(x_t, y_t)}{\sum_{\tilde{y}} \exp f(x_t, \tilde{y})}, \tag{2}$$

where W_y is the model parameter.

In sequence labeling formalization, there is a strong dependency between labels. For example, the label before $I - t_1$ must be either $B - t_1$ or $I - t_1$. Conditional Random Field [8] (CRF) introduces an additional transition matrix A to model this dependency explicitly. So the conditional probability becomes:

$$g(x_t, y', y) = W_y^\top \mathbf{h}_t + A_{y',y}, \tag{3}$$

$$\text{score}(\mathbf{x}, \mathbf{y}) = \sum_{t=1}^{T} g(x_t, y_{t-1}, y_t), \tag{4}$$

$$p(\mathbf{y}|\mathbf{x}) = \frac{\exp(\text{score}(\mathbf{x}, \mathbf{y}))}{\sum_{\tilde{\mathbf{y}}} \exp(\text{score}(\mathbf{x}, \tilde{\mathbf{y}}))}, \tag{5}$$

where $W_y^\top \mathbf{h}_t, A_{y',y}$ are generally referred to as the emission score and the transition score, respectively.

Despite simplicity, CRF is superior to linear classifiers in terms of the model performance, so it becomes the mainstream sequence labeling solution currently.

3.2   Voting-Based Multi-teacher Knowledge Transfer

In order to aggregate the knowledge from multiple data sources $X_1, X_2, ..., X_n$ into a single model, a straightforward idea is to first merge all the data from different sources, and then train a complete model $m(\cdot, \hat{\theta})$ on the merged data. This process can be formalized as follows:

$$X_\cup = \bigcup_{i=1}^{n} X_i, \tag{6}$$

$$\hat{\theta} = \arg\min_{\theta} \mathcal{L}(X_\cup, m(\cdot; \theta)), \tag{7}$$

where $\mathcal{L}$ is the loss function.

However, clinical data is often sensitive and cannot be shared, and existing studies [1,5,14,16] have shown that this training method has a serious risk of privacy leakage. In order to protect the privacy, Papernot et al. [12] proposed Private Aggregation of Teacher Ensembles (PATE), divided into three steps:

(1) Train teacher models separately on each dataset, namely

$$\hat{\theta}_i = \arg\min_{\theta} \mathcal{L}(X_i, m(\cdot; \theta))). \tag{8}$$

(2) Generate a pseudo-label for each element in the unlabeled and non-sensitive transfer set X_{transfer} through teachers' voting.
(3) Train the student model on the label-generated transfer set.

Under this aggregation strategy, the training of the student model does not directly use sensitive data. Instead, it is completed by imitating the prediction of teacher models on non-sensitive data, which protects the privacy of sensitive data.

3.3   Knowledge Distillation

Voting, a simple and direct aggregation method, has disadvantages such as loss of prediction details of the teacher. Hinton et al. [7] proposed knowledge distillation, that is, training the student under the supervision of the teacher's logits. Specifically, given the logit z^s and z^t output by the student and the teacher, the distillation loss $\mathcal{L}_{KD}$ could be calculated as:

$$p^s = \text{softmax}(z^S/T), \tag{9}$$

$$p^t = \text{softmax}(z^T/T), \tag{10}$$

$$\mathcal{L}_{KD} = \text{KL}(p^t||p^s), \tag{11}$$

where T is the temperature, which determines the smoothness of the probability distribution; KL is the Kullback-Leibler Divergence [9].

4   Methodology

4.1   Framework Overview

The multi-teacher distillation framework is shown in Fig. 1. The training of this framework consists of three main steps:

(1) For every dataset X_i in $\{X_1, X_2, \cdots, X_n\}$, train a teacher model m_i;
(2) Utilize every teacher model m_i in $\{m_1, m_2, \cdots, m_n\}$ to produce the probability distribution $p^{t(i)}$ for the transfer set X_{transfer};
(3) Align $p^{t(i)}$ with the student model's predictions, and then iteratively update the parameters of the student model with the distillation loss.

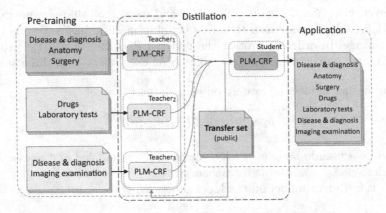

Fig. 1. The framework of the proposed privacy knowledge transfer method. PLM denotes Pre-trained Language model, which is utilized as a language encoder.

Section 4.2 describes the sequence knowledge distillation method, which is employed to calculate the distillation loss. Section 4.3 introduces how to align the probability distributions produced by the teacher model and the student model.

4.2   Sequence Distillation

Word-Level Distillation. Knowledge distillation enables knowledge transfer between two models by fitting their soft labels. When the sequence labeling solution is a linear classifier, the soft label is the probability distribution output by the classifier at each position of the sequence; when the solution is CRF, the soft label is the emission probability. Given a sequence $\mathbf{x} = [x_1, x_2, ..., x_T]$, let z_{tj} be the score of v_j being the label of x_t, then the corresponding soft label $p(y_t|x)$ can be calculated as follows:

$$p(y_t = v_j|\mathbf{x}) = \frac{\exp(z_{tj}/T)}{\sum_{k=1}^{|V|} \exp(z_{tk}/T)}, \tag{12}$$

where V is the label space and T is the temperature. The higher the temperature, the smoother the soft label obtained.

The word-level knowledge distillation method is to minimize the difference between the label probability distribution output by teachers and the student to realize the training of the student model. The loss function is:

$$\mathcal{L}_{\text{word}}(p^t, p^s) = -\sum_{t=1}^{T} \sum_{j=1}^{|V|} p^t(y_t = v_j | \mathbf{x}) \log p^s(y_t = v_j | \mathbf{x}), \tag{13}$$

where $p^t(y_i|x)$ and $p^s(y_i|x)$ are the label probability distribution produced by the teacher and the student respectively.

Sequence-Level Distillation. Since the word-level distillation does not take the connection between labels into consideration, its ability to model the structural information of the sequence is weak. Therefore, the target of the sequence-level distillation method is the posterior probability fusing the entire label sequence information, instead of the emission probability at each position. The posterior probability $q(y_t|\mathbf{x})$ is defined from the perspective of probability decomposition:

$$p(y_1, y_2, \cdots, y_T | \mathbf{x}) = \sum_{t=1}^{T} q(y_t | \mathbf{x}), \tag{14}$$

$$q(y_t | \mathbf{x}) = \sum_{\{y_1, y_2, \cdots, y_T\} \backslash y_t} p(y_1, y_2, \cdots, y_T | \mathbf{x}). \tag{15}$$

$q(y_t|\mathbf{x})$ can be further computed as follows:

$$q(y_t | \mathbf{x}) \propto \alpha(y_t) \times \beta(y_t), \tag{16}$$

$$\alpha(y_t) = \sum_{y_1, y_2, \cdots, y_{t-1}} \exp\left(\sum_{k=1}^{t} g(x_k, y_{k-1}, y_k)\right), \tag{17}$$

$$\beta(y_t) = \sum_{y_{t+1}, \cdots, y_T} \exp\left(\sum_{k=t+1}^{T} g(x_k, y_{k-1}, y_k)\right), \tag{18}$$

where $\alpha(y_t)$ and $\beta(y_t)$ are forward variable and backward variable respectively, calculated by forward algorithm and backward algorithm [2].

Therefore, the loss of sequence-level distillation is:

$$\mathcal{L}_{seq}(q^t, p^s) = -\sum_{t=1}^{T} \sum_{j=1}^{|V|} q^t(y_t = v_j | x) \log q^s(y_t = v_j | x) \tag{19}$$

In subsequent experiments, we could find that combining word-level and sequence-level distillation led to the better performance.

4.3 Heterogeneous Knowledge Aggregation

In practice, the label spaces of teachers and the student are often heterogeneous. This is because the label sets of data from different sources are often different, and the label set of the student model is supposed to contain all the labels. Formally, let the label set corresponding to the ith teacher be V_i, then the label set corresponding to the student model should be

$$V_\cup = \bigcup_i V_i. \qquad (20)$$

When the teachers and the student are heterogeneous, the loss function mentioned in Sect. 4.2 can not be applied directly, because for $v \in V_\cup \backslash V_i$, $p^{t(i)}(y_t = v)$ (as well as $q^{t(i)}(y_t = v)$) is undefined. A naive solution is to set $p^{t(i)}(y_t = v) = 0$, However, it introduces erroneous supervision information, leading to the poor utility of the subsequent model.

Re-normalization Operation. In order to overcome the heterogeneity issue, we re-normalize the label probability output by the student model to align with the label sets of the teachers. Suppose the label probability produced by the student model is $p^s(y_t|\mathbf{x})$, then the normalized label probability is

$$p^{s(i)}(y_t = v|\mathbf{x}) = \frac{p^s(y_t = v|\mathbf{x})}{\sum_{\tilde{v} \in V_i} p^s(y_t = \tilde{v}|\mathbf{x})}. \qquad (21)$$

After this alignment, the distillation loss between the ith teacher and the student can be calculated by:

$$\mathcal{L}_{kd}(p^s, p^{t(i)}) = -\sum_{t=1}^{T} \sum_{v \in V_i} p^{t(i)}(y_t = v|\mathbf{x}) \log p^{s(i)}(y_t = v|\mathbf{x}). \qquad (22)$$

Weight Adjustment Strategy. In addition to the heterogeneity issue, there is category bias in multi-teacher aggregation. Since certain categories appear in most teachers' label space, the student model will be biased towards these categories. In order to eliminate the category bias, we introduce a weight for each category when calculating the loss function:

$$\mathcal{L}_{kd}(i) = -\sum_{t=1}^{T} \sum_{v \in V_i} w(v) \times p^{t(i)}(y_t = v|\mathbf{x}) \log p^{s(i)}(y_t = v|\mathbf{x}), \qquad (23)$$

where $w(v)$ is the reciprocal of the average $p(y_t = v)$:

$$w(v) = \frac{nT}{\sum_{t=1}^{T} \sum_{i=1}^{n} p^{t(i)}(y_t = v)}. \qquad (24)$$

where n is the number of the teachers.

5 Experiment

5.1 Dataset

We evaluate our method on the Chinese GLUE Chinese electronic medical text record entity recognition dataset [17], hereafter referred to as the Chinese GLUE dataset. This dataset was published by Chinese GLUE[1] and constructed by Yidu Cloud (Beijing) Technology[2], containing 6 categories of entities. The specific statistical information is shown in Table 1. Table 2 shows a sample from the dataset.

Table 1. Statistics of Chinese GLUE dataset.

Split	Train	Test
#sentence	1000	379

Table 2. An sample of Chinese GLUE dataset.

Text	患者3月前因"直肠癌"于在我院于全麻上行直肠癌根治术
	The patient underwent transanal endoscopic microsurgery under general anesthesia in our hospital 3 months ago due to "rectal cancer"
Entity	直肠癌(疾病和诊断), 直肠癌根治手术(手术)
	rectal cancer (disease & diagnosis), transanal endoscopic microsurgery (surgery)

In order to simulate the scenario of multiple data sources, we divide the original data set X horizontally to obtain n disjoint subsets $\{X_i, ..., X_n\}$. In addition, we set aside a part of the original test set as the transfer set. The statistical information of the divided dataset is shown in Table 3.

Table 3. Dataset division for multi-source scenario.

Split	Train-i X_i	Transfer	Test
#sentence	100–300	200	179

---

[1] http://www.cluebenchmark.com/.
[2] https://www.yiducloud.com.cn/.

5.2 Experiment Settings

We choose the BERT model [3] as the language encoder and initialize it with chinese-roberta-wwm-ext[3]. We utilize CRF as the default solution for sequence labeling. The maximum sentence length is set to 256. The optimizer we adopt is the adam optimizer [4] with the learning rate of $1e-4$ and the batch size of 16, and the early stop strategy are applied. This paper evaluates the performance of our method by precision, recall, and F1-measure.

5.3 Results and Analysis

Results on Sequence Distillation. For sequence labeling task, two possible solutions are linear classifier and conditional random fields, denoted as BERT-softmax and BERT-CRF, respectively. Demonstrated as Table 4, BERT-CRF outperforms BERT-Softmax, indicating that the modeling ability of CRF is better. For sequence distillation, it can be found that the sequence-level distillation shows better performance than the word-level distillation, and the best performance is obtained by combining the two. As Table 4 shown, our distillation method can obtain a student with similar performance to the teacher in the single-source scenario, with less than 7 ‰ drop in F1-measure.

Table 4. Experimental results in the single-source scenario.

Method		Precision	Recall	F1
Teacher	BERT-softmax	0.8799	0.7792	0.8265
	BERT-CRF	**0.8819**	**0.7887**	**0.8327**
Student	Word-level	0.8736	0.7625	0.8143
	Sequence-level	**0.8783**	0.7791	0.8257
	Ensemble	0.8764	**0.7811**	**0.8260**

Results on Knowledge Aggregation. Table 5 shows the performance of the proposed knowledge transfer method in the multi-source scenario. It can be found that the performance of the model obtained by direct distillation of multiple heterogeneous teachers is rather low, only 0.6289, which has a large gap with the fully supervised method. Re-normalization operation improves the performance of the distilled model significantly, which manifests the necessity of label space alignment. With weight adjustment strategy, this performance improves further. Compared with the fully supervised method, the proposed privacy knowledge aggregation method has only less than 1% drop in F1-measure, which demonstrates the strong practicality of our method.

---

[3] https://github.com/ymcui/Chinese-BERT-wwm

Table 5. Experimental results in the multi-source scenario. "norm" denotes the re-normalization operation, and "weight" denotes the weight adjustment strategy.

Method	Precision	Recall	F1
Fully-supervised	0.8819	0.7887	0.8327
Distilled model	0.8773	0.4901	0.6289
+ norm	0.8782	0.7725	0.8190
+ norm & weight	**0.8789**	**0.7746**	**0.8235**

Furthermore, we list the performance of the teachers and the student on different entity categories in Table 6. The performance of the student on disease & diagnosis and anatomy surpasses all teachers, since there is knowledge transfer from all teachers and the student is trained fully. While on the other categories, because only one teacher has the category annotated, the student is trained inadequately and consequently there is a large gap between the performance of the student and the teachers.

Table 6. Models' performance in each category.

Method	疾病和诊断 disease & diagnosis	解剖部位 anatomy	手术 surgery	影响检查 image examination	药物 drugs	实验室检验 lab tests
Teacher1	77.33	81.79	**74.29**	–	–	–
Teacher2	78.96	–	–	**83.27**	–	–
Teacher3	83.85	78.06	–	–	**93.68**	**62.60**
Student	**85.69**	**83.22**	66.10	70.59	88.69	52.71

6   Conclusion

This paper proposes a privacy knowledge transfer method to address the privacy leakage issue in deep learning models. For the scenario where the training data is from multiple sources and heterogeneous, we introduce the re-normalization operation and weight adjustment strategy. In order to verify the effectiveness of the proposed method, we conduct experiments on a clinical concept extraction task, and the experiment results show that the models obtained by our method can achieve comparable results with the fully supervised method.

Acknowledgement. This work was partially supported by National Key Research and Development Program of China (2017YFB0802204), National Natural Science Foundation of China (61876053, 62006062), Shenzhen Foundational Research Funding (JCYJ20180507183527919 and JCYJ20200109113441941).

References

1. Carlini, N., et al.: Extracting training data from large language models. arXiv preprint arXiv:2012.07805 (2020)
2. Devijver, P.A.: Baum's forward-backward algorithm revisited. Pattern Recogn. Lett. **3**(6), 369–373 (1985)
3. Devlin, J., Chang, M.W., Lee, K., Toutanova, K.: BERT: pre-training of deep bidirectional transformers for language understanding. In: Proceedings of the 2019 Conference of the North American Chapter of the Association for Computational Linguistics: Human Language Technologies, Volume 1 (Long and Short Papers), pp. 4171–4186 (2019)
4. Kingma, D.P., Ba, J.L.: Adam: a method for stochastic optimizaiton. In: Proceedings of the 3rd International Conference for Learning Representations (2015)
5. Fredrikson, M., Jha, S., Ristenpart, T.: Model inversion attacks that exploit confidence information and basic countermeasures, pp. 1322–1333 (10 2015). https://doi.org/10.1145/2810103.2813677
6. Fu, S., et al.: Development of clinical concept extraction applications: a methodology review. CoRR abs/1910.11377 (2019). http://arxiv.org/abs/1910.11377
7. Hinton, G., Dean, J., Vinyals, O.: Distilling the knowledge in a neural network, pp. 1–9, March 2014
8. John Lafferty, A.M., Pereira, F.C.: Conditional random fields: probabilistic models for segmenting and labeling sequence data. In: Proceedings of the 18th International Conference on Machine Learning, pp. 282–289 (2001)
9. Kullback, S.: Information Theory and Statistics. Courier Corporation (1997)
10. Lopes, R.G., Fenu, S., Starner, T.: Data-free knowledge distillation for deep neural networks. CoRR abs/1710.07535 (2017)
11. Nadeau, D., Sekine, S.: A survey of named entity recognition and classification. Lingvisticæ Invest. **30**(1), 3–26 (2007). https://doi.org/10.1075/li.30.1.03nad, https://www.jbe-platform.com/content/journals/10.1075/li.30.1.03nad
12. Papernot, N., Abadi, M., Erlingsson, Ú., Goodfellow, I., Talwar, K.: Semi-supervised knowledge transfer for deep learning from private training data (2017)
13. Ross, A.S., Doshi-Velez, F.: Improving the adversarial robustness and interpretability of deep neural networks by regularizing their input gradients. In: McIlraith, S.A., Weinberger, K.Q. (eds.) Proceedings of the Thirty-Second AAAI Conference on Artificial Intelligence, (AAAI-18), the 30th Innovative Applications of Artificial Intelligence (IAAI-18), and the 8th AAAI Symposium on Educational Advances in Artificial Intelligence (EAAI-18), New Orleans, Louisiana, USA, 2–7 February 2018, pp. 1660–1669. AAAI Press (2018)
14. Shokri, R., Stronati, M., Song, C., Shmatikov, V.: Membership inference attacks against machine learning models. In: 2017 IEEE Symposium on Security and Privacy (SP), pp. 3–18. IEEE (2017)
15. Wang, Y., et al.: Clinical information extraction applications: a literature review. J. Biomed. Inf. **77**, 34–49 (2018). https://doi.org/10.1016/j.jbi.2017.11.011, https://www.sciencedirect.com/science/article/pii/S1532046417302563
16. Yeom, S., Giacomelli, I., Fredrikson, M., Jha, S.: Privacy risk in machine learning: analyzing the connection to overfitting, pp. 268–282, July 2018. https://doi.org/10.1109/CSF.2018.00027
17. Zhao, J., Van Harmelen, F., Tang, J., Han, X., Wang, Q., Li, X.: Knowledge Graph and Semantic Computing. Knowledge Computing and Language Understanding: Third China Conference, CCKS 2018, Tianjin, China, August 14–17, 2018, Revised Selected Papers, vol. 957. Springer, Singapore (2018). https://doi.org/10.1007/978-981-13-3146-6

Multimodal Social Media Sentiment Analysis Based on Cross-Modal Hierarchical Attention Fusion

Kezhong Wang and Ting Jin(✉)

Hainan University, Haikou 570228, People's Republic of China
19081200210010@hainanu.edu.cn, tingj@fudan.edu.cn

Abstract. With the diversification of data forms on social media, more and more multimodal information mixed with image and text replaces the traditional single text description. Compared with single-modal data, multimodal data can more fully express people's opinions, and it also contains richer emotional information. Therefore, the task of multimodal sentiment analysis is gradually becoming a hot topic of current research. However, images and texts do not always complement each other in expressing emotional polarity in real social media. Moreover, the contribution of different modal information to the overall emotional polarity is also different. To solve these problems, a multimodal sentiment analysis method (CMHAF) that integrates topic information is proposed. The method first extracts topical information that highly summarizes the comment content from social media texts. Secondly, the current outstanding pre-training models are used to obtain emotional features of various modalities. And then, we propose cross-modal global fusion and cross-modal high-level semantic fusion methods to combine the features of different levels. At last, we conduct extensive experiments on a real Chinese multimodal dataset. The experimental results show that compared with the baseline method, the proposed method has significant improvement in multiple indicators, and can effectively classify the sentiment of multimodal social media reviews.

Keywords: Social media · Multimodal sentiment analysis · Topic information · Cross-modal fusion

1 Introduction

In recent years, with the rapid development of the Internet and the widespread popularity of mobile devices, people have become accustomed to using social media software to express their views on events and share their experiences. Moreover, the forms of data on social media platforms are becoming more and more diverse. Compared with the early days when people could only use a single text message to express their opinions, now people prefer to use multimodal information to express their emotions. For example, people on social platforms usually attach one or more pictures to the text content to enhance their expression. Figure 1 shows the multimodal comments on Twitter and

Y. Pan et al. (Eds.): AIMS 2021, LNCS 12987, pp. 29–44, 2022.
https://doi.org/10.1007/978-3-030-96033-9_3

Weibo. Multimodal data can contain more information and express more comprehensive emotions than single text data. The task of multimodal sentiment analysis is gradually attracting more and more attention in recent years [1, 2]. Therefore, some different fusion methods for multimodal information have been proposed, such as early fusion [3, 4], intermediate fusion [5–7], and late fusion [8, 9].

However, most of the existing sentiment analysis methods only consider a single modality of text [10, 11] or image [12, 13]. If we only study the single modal emotion, we can't accurately express the emotional polarity of multimodal information. Therefore, sentiment analysis [14] on multimodal data is becoming a current trend. In fact, comments with irrelevant images and texts are very common in real social media. Due to the abstractness of the image in expressing emotions, it is easy to introduce noise signals by fusing multimodal information directly. Besides, some works do not fully consider the correlation between images and texts. So how to fully excavate the emotional features in different modalities and effectively integrate cross-modal features has become difficult points in current research. Thus, although the task of multimodal sentiment analysis is becoming more and more important, the study of sentiment analysis based on multimodal information still faces many challenges.

Oh yes, we did. #vegan   因为有了你们这个冬
#cheese #Toronto vegan   天很温暖！#致敬白衣
#food #organic#   战士#武汉加油

Fig. 1. Two examples of social media comments. The first one is from Twitter and the second is from Weibo.

Therefore, in order to solve the above problems in the research of multimodal sentiment analysis, this paper proposes a multimodal sentiment analysis method (CMHAF) that integrates topic semantic information and two cross-modal fusion methods. The main contributions of this paper include the following three aspects:

1) We propose a multimodal sentiment analysis method (CMHAF) that integrates topic information.
2) We focus on multimodal feature fusion from two levels to further explore the internal relationship between image and text. Furthermore, a cross-modal global feature fusion method and a cross-modal high-level semantic fusion method are introduced to combine different levels of features.
3) The experimental results on a Chinese social comment dataset show that the multimodal sentiment analysis model we proposed has a great improvement in many

indicators compared with the baseline model. Moreover, the ablation experiment proves that the topic information can effectively improve the classification effect.

2 Related Work

2.1 Text Sentiment Analysis

Text sentiment analysis has always been a hot research task in the field of natural language processing. Thanks to the remarkable achievements of deep learning in NLP in recent years, a variety of neural networks have been widely used in the research on text sentiment analysis. For example, [15, 16] used convolutional neural network CNN to achieve sentiment classification tasks. [17] used RNN and [18, 19] used LSTM to perform sentiment analysis on texts. Moreover, this work [20] used a hybrid neural network.

Previously, people just applied the attention mechanism to the computer vision field. In addition, although the attention mechanism [21] was first proposed in the field of vision, later [22] applied the attention mechanism to machine translation tasks. Moreover, the proposal of transformer [23] allows a variety of attention mechanisms [24] to be used in NLP tasks. The addition of attention mechanism further improves the performance of the model.

In recent years, a series of pre-trained language models have been proposed, such as ELMo [25], BERT [26], GPT [27], and so on. These pre-trained language models trained in advance on large-scale corpus have achieved SOTA results in a variety of NLP tasks. They have contributed greatly to the advancement of the field of NLP, as well as the development of textual sentiment analysis techniques. However, most of the current social comments are a mix of texts, images, and even videos. If we only research text sentiment analysis, we often can't fully show the true feelings of users.

2.2 Image Sentiment Analysis

Because the emotion of the image is abstract and subjective, the image sentiment analysis is not as simple and effective as the text. In the early days, people used low-level features [12] in image sentiment analysis tasks. Compared with low-level features, middle-level features [28–30] can better reflect the emotions expressed by the image. Moreover, [29] constructed 1200 image adjective-noun pairs (ANP) to classify images. [30] introduced a topic model, which enhances the classification performance by considering the topic categories of different pictures.

With the rapid development of deep learning technology, more methods [12, 31, 32] use deep neural networks. In addition, a variety of pre-training models have been proposed, such as VGG [33], ResNet [34], and DenseNet [35]. These deep convolution models pre-trained on ImageNet have shown powerful performance in image classification tasks. After all, image information is abstract in the expression of emotions. The accuracy of the methods only based on comment images is not ideal.

2.3 Multimodal Sentiment Analysis

In recent years, thanks to the rapid development of social media, multimodal sentiment analysis has become an emerging and hot area. Both academia and industry have
found that it has great research value, and more current methods [36, 37] are based
on deep learning. [7] proposed a Deep Multimodal Attentive Fusion (DMAF) method
for image-text sentiment analysis which outperforms state-of-the-art baselines on four
real-world datasets. [38] presented a Visual Aspect Attention Network (VistaNet), which
takes images as visual attention to emphasize important information in sentence text.
[39] used Multi-Interactive Memory Network (MIMN) to capture the interactive information between multi-modality and single-modality for aspect-level and multimodal
sentiment analysis. [40] proposed a hierarchical fusion method that integrates image,
attribute, and text features to address the challenging multi-modal sarcasm detection
task. In addition, more fusion methods are currently using feature splicing or attention
mechanism. But [41] proposed a Tensor Fusion Network (TFN) to capture single-mode
internal information and cross-modal interaction information.

When dealing with multimodal information, although the feature extraction of
modals is very important, multimodal fusion is still a key step. Currently, multimodal
fusion methods can be divided into three categories. Although the original information
of each mode is retained in the early fusion, the dimensions of the fused vector will be
too high and contain unnecessary redundant information. Late fusion is easier to achieve,
but it does not consider the correlation between cross-modalities. Hybrid fusion combines the advantages of the first two methods, but the fusion model is more complicated
and the difficulty of training will be greater. Even, the different modes are sometimes
strongly correlated with each other and sometimes semantically unrelated. It is a thorny
problem that how to effectively integrate the semantic features of the modes and consider
the contribution of the modes to the judgment of emotional polarity. Thus, it can be seen
that there are still many serious challenges to be overcome in the task of multimodal
sentiment analysis.

3 Proposed Multimodal Sentiment Analysis Approach

In this section, we will describe the proposed model CMHAF in more detail. The overall
structure of the model is shown in Fig. 2. We first extract topic information from the text
and take image, topic, and text as three modalities. In order to fully obtain the emotional
information within the modal, we use pre-training models to extract features. Then, the
topic information is used to construct high-level semantic connections between images
and texts. The proposed hierarchical attention fusion methodcan effectively combine the
features on the corresponding levels of image and text modals. Finally, the multimodal
fusion features are used to classify the emotions.

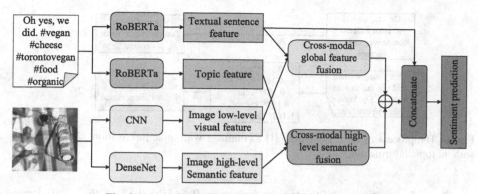

Fig. 2. The overall architecture of the proposed model.

3.1 Feature Extraction

Our proposed model has three modal information as input. The feature extraction methods for each modal will be provided as follow.

Text Feature Extraction

Text comments on social media often contain some special symbols and useless information. Before these texts are sent into the model, they need to be preprocessed to delete the useless information. Since the pre-training model shows strong text representation ability in NLP tasks, we use the current popular Bert and Roberta model to encode the texts. And the output vector [CLS] is used as the emotional feature of texts.

We define a set of n texts in the dataset as $W = \{W_1, W_2, \ldots, W_i, \ldots, W_n\}$, where n denotes the number of comments. And we obtain the vector representation $S = \{S_1, S_2, \ldots, S_i, \ldots, S_n\}$ of the text by encoding the sentences with Bert as follows:

$$S_i = RoBERTa(W_i) \tag{1}$$

where S_i is the feature vector of the text modal.

Topic Feature Extraction

Whether on Weibo or Twitter, text comments often contain topical information. These words are generally the core of the whole review and are more similar to the image semantics. Therefore, we extract topic information from the review text to construct high-level semantic connections between graphic and text modalities. The specific process of topic extraction is shown in Fig. 3. For comments that contain topic information, we choose to intercept them directly. For comments without topic information, we use the LDA topic model to extract topic words. The first five words of confidence are extracted from the comment text as the topic information.

After getting the topic information, we feed them into the model as input. The topic information is also in the form of text, so we still use the same pre-trained models BERT and RoBERTa as above to extract topic features:

$$T_i = RoBERTa(P_i) \tag{2}$$

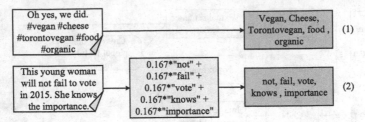

Fig. 3. The process of topic extraction: (1) a comment with topic information; (2) a comment without topic information.

where P_i denotes one of the topic information $P = \{P_1, P_2, \ldots, P_i, \ldots, P_n\}$ and T_i is the topic feature vector.

Image Feature Extraction

Since the expression of emotion is abstract rather than intuitive in images, it is not accurate to extract only single visual features for image sentiment analysis. Different from some existing works, we extract two levels of image features: low-level visual features and high-level semantic features.

The module which consists of four convolution layers and four global max-pooling layers is constructed to obtain low-level visual features of the images, e.g. color, edge, and texture. Let $I = \{I_1, I_2, \ldots, I_i, \ldots, I_n\}$ denotes a set of n images. We can get the low-level visual representation I_i^l of the image I_i by feeding it through the constructed model:

$$I_i^l = CNN(I_i) \tag{3}$$

We migrate the model parameters of DenseNet121 pre-trained on ImageNet to our task. Then the final fully-connected layer used for image classification is modified into a feature mapping layer to extract high-level semantic features of the image as follows:

$$DI_i^h = DenseNet121(I_i) \tag{4}$$

$$I_i^h = MLP(DI_i^h) \tag{5}$$

where DI_i^h is the feature vector obtained by DenseNet121 and I_i^h is the high-level semantic features.

3.2 Cross-Modal Global Feature Fusion

We assume that there is often semantic independence between the text and the image, so directly fusing the multimodal features may produce noise and affect the classification performance of the model. To solve this problem, we first propose a cross-modal global feature fusion method to combine the sentence representation of the text with the low-level visual features of the image. The cross-modal global feature representation is constructed by fusing the whole emotional information of multimodal.

We combine the sentence feature S_i of the text with the low-level visual feature I_i^l of the image by vector concatenate. Then we use the self-attention mechanism to highlight the important information in the fusion feature vector:

$$C_i = Concatenate(I_i^l, S_i) \qquad (6)$$

$$Att_i^l = Self - attention(C_i) \qquad (7)$$

where C_i is the concatenated vector and Att_i^l is a low-level attention feature of image-text after the self-attention mechanism. Finally, a fully-connected layer is used to obtain cross-modal global fusion features G_i:

$$G_i = MLP(Att_i^l) \qquad (8)$$

3.3 Cross-Modal High-Level Semantic Fusion

In order to further explore the internal relationship between image and text, we propose a cross-modal high-level semantic fusion method to combine the high-level semantic features of the image and the topic features of the text. The architecture of cross-modal high-level semantic fusion is shown in Fig. 4 and the more detailed process is described below.

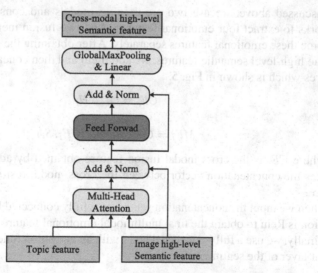

Fig. 4. The architecture of cross-modal high-level semantic fusion.

We regard topic features of text as Key and Value in the self-attention mechanism, and high-level semantic features of images as Query in the self-attention mechanism. By using the high-level semantic features of the image to guide the topic features for vector calculation, more weight is assigned to the words related to the image semantics in the topic features. Then we get the image-text high-level semantic attention feature Att_i^h. The detailed formula is as follows:

$$Att_i^h = Attention(T_j, I_i^h) \tag{9}$$

After attention calculation, we use a structure similar to Transformer to get the fusion feature F_i^h:

$$N_i^h = LN\left(Att_i^h \oplus I_i^h\right) \tag{10}$$

$$N_i^h = LN\left(Att_i^h \oplus I_i^h\right) \tag{11}$$

$$F_i^h = LN\left(M_i^h \oplus N_i^h\right) \tag{12}$$

where $\oplus$ represents vector addition, LN is residual connection, and MLP is feedforward connection layer. Finally, a global max pooling layer and a fully connected layer are used to obtain the high-level semantic features of the image and text:

$$O_i = GlobalMaxPooling(F_i^h) \tag{13}$$

$$H_i = MLP(O_i) \tag{14}$$

3.4 Sentiment Classification

As discussed above, we use two pre-training models and constructed convolutional networks to extract four emotional features. And two fusion methods are proposed to combine these emotional features separately. After obtaining the global fusion features and the high-level semantic features, we add them and then concatenate them with text features which is shown in Fig. 5.

$$CF_i = G_i \oplus H_i \tag{15}$$

$$MF_i = Concatenate(CF_i, S_i) \tag{16}$$

where CF_i is the cross-modal fusion feature obtained by adding G_i and H_i; MF_i denotes the concatenation vector between the cross-modal fusion feature and the text feature.

Then we input the concatenation vectors to a fully connected layer whose activation function is Relu to obtain the final multimodal emotional feature representation.

Finally, we use a fully-connected layer with an activation function of softmax as the output layer of the sentiment category:

$$M_i = MLP(MF_i) \tag{17}$$

$$p_i = softmax(M_i \cdot W + b) \tag{18}$$

where M_i denotes the multimodal feature vectors which is ready to serve as input of the output layer; p_i denotes the probability distribution of the final sentiment classification; W is weight matric and b is bias.

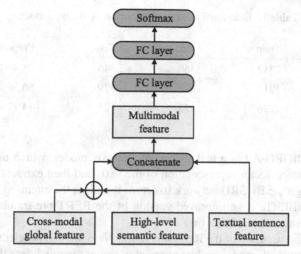

Fig. 5. The architecture of the multimodal sentiment classification.

4 Experiments

In this section, we introduce our experimental dataset firstly. And then the baselines and experimental settings are depicted. Finally, we present experimental results and evaluate the performance of our model by performing an ablation analysis. In addition, we add a case study to further analyze the workings of the model.

4.1 Datasets

In this work, we use a multimodal social media dataset Weibo comments. The statistics of the experimental dataset are shown in Table 1. Here, we give a brief introduction to the above dataset.

At present, there are few Chinese social media datasets for multimodal sentiment analysis tasks, so we use image-text pairs crawled from Sina Weibo as the Chinese multimodal dataset. Since the number of pictures corresponding to each comment text is not the same, we only keep the comments containing one picture to facilitate the experiment and research. The text content on Weibo comments usually contains some useless information and special symbols, so it is necessary to delete duplicate data, data with incomplete information, and useless information. Finally, we obtain 9765 image-text weibos and each review has only one image. The distribution of emotion labels in the Weibo dataset is shown in Table 1.

4.2 Baselines

In order to verify the performance of our model CMHAF, we compare the model with the single-modal sentiment analysis model and the existing multimodal sentiment analysis model.

Table 1. Emotional polarity distribution of Weibo dataset.

Label	Train	Val	Test	Proportion
Positive	2782	366	346	35.47%
Neutral	3913	476	529	50.36%
Negative	1126	132	125	14.17%

- BiGRU-Att. BiGRU-Att is a text sentiment analysis model, which uses Word2Vec to obtain the word vector representation of the text, and then extracts the sentiment features through the Bi-GRU network structure based on the attention mechanism.
- RoBERTa. RoBERTa is an improved version of the BERT pre-training model, and further pre-training for Chinese data.
- ResNet101. The structure of the Residual Neural Network can accelerate the training of the neural network model, and its parameter amount is much less than that of the VGG network. Moreover, ResNet can also solve gradient disappearance and gradient explosion to a certain extent.
- DenseNet121. DenseNet is a densely connected convolutional neural network with a deeper number of layers. Compared with ResNet, it has fewer parameters, strengthens the reuse of features, and can also solve the problem of gradient disappearance to a certain extent.
- TFN. A multi-modal fusion method based on tensor outer product combines single-modal and cross-modal representation vectors.
- RoBERTa-ResNet [42]. The RoBERTa and ResNet pre-training models are used to extract the emotional features in the text and images respectively. Then the two modal features are directly fused to obtain a multi-modal feature representation. Finally, the fused features are classified into emotions.
- RoBERTa-DenseNet [42]. This model is similar to RoBERTa-ResNet. Only the image features are extracted by DenseNet.
- RoBERTa-CNN. This model is also similar to RoBERTa-ResNet. Only the image features are extracted by CNN.

4.3 Experimental Settings

For the text modal, we use RoBERTa-zh-base to extract Chinese text features, and BERT-base to extract English text features. The maximum length of the text description is set to 160. Those less than 160 are filled with 0 at the back end, and those more than 160 are truncated at the back end. The processing of topic information is similar to the above, except that the maximum length is set to 20. For the image modal, the input size of the image is 224×224. We use the pre-trained model Densenet121 for high-level feature extraction and construct CNN model to extract global features.

In training, we use Adam for gradient-based optimization with a batch size of 4 and use the categorical cross-entropy loss for the loss function. The training set, validation set, and test set are divided approximately 8:1:1. The training epoch is set to 10, and the Early Stopping strategy is used to prevent training from overfitting. Moreover, we keep the model with the highest accuracy on the validation set after training and adjusting the hyper-parameters many times. For a fair comparison, we report the average results on the test sets. And In addition, our experiments are run on an Nvidia 2080Ti GPU, and our code is based on the Keras deep learning framework of Tensorflow.

In order to evaluate the performance of the model, we select various evaluation metrics: accuracy, precision, and recall. Further, due to the imbalance of the label categories in the datasets, we also introduce F1-Score as an important metric.

4.4 Experimental Results

In Table 2, we show the experimental results on the dataset of Weibo. It can be concluded that our model outperforms the baseline models on four metrics. Our proposed model CMHAF achieves 79.1% accuracy which represents a 2.3% improvement upon TFN. Especially, the average F1 of 75.14% represents a 3.17% improvement upon RoBERTa-DenseNet. Therefore, our proposed model can perform better in the face of category imbalance.

Table 2. Experimental results on Weibo dataset.

Model	Precision	Recall	F1	Accuracy
BiGRU-Att	0.6948	0.6863	0.6863	0.7487
RoBERTa	0.7156	0.7279	0.7156	0.7680
ResNet101	0.5399	0.5223	0.5277	0.6140
DenseNet121	0.5647	0.5556	0.5595	0.6410
TFN	0.7193	0.7462	0.7302	0.7680
RoBERTa-ResNet	0.7233	0.7170	0.7197	0.7690
RoBERTa-DenseNet	0.7369	0.7303	0.7329	0.7800
RoBERTa-CNN	0.7382	0.7435	0.7408	0.7750
CMHAF	**0.7542**	**0.7516**	**0.7514**	**0.7910**

In addition, when performing a single modal sentiment analysis task, the text models perform much better than image models. This also confirms our view that text modal contributes more to sentiment analysis than image modal.

Compared with the single modal models, the multimodal models that combine image and text features are overall improved. Interestingly, the models that only combine text features with low-level visual features outperform some other multi-modal models in multiple metrics. This may be due to the fact that the semantics of the texts and the images are not related, so the high-level semantic features of the image are not helpful to the model.

4.5 Ablation Analysis

To study the importance of multimodal information and the contribution of each module, we conduct ablation analysis experiments. By combining image, text, and topic modal and model composition, the effectiveness of the proposed method is further verified. The detailed experimental results are shown in Table 3. The T/P/V indicates the existence of the text(T), topic(P), and visual (V) modalities and CMHF represents the model without the proposed attention fusion methods.

We start from the most basic text model and gradually increase the composition of the model. From Table 3, it is easy to see that among the three modalities, text plays the most important role, followed by topic information and abstract image. We can also find that the text model added topic features has improved overall metrics than the text single modal model. Especially, we improve F1-score by 2.02% as compared to the text model. This shows that the topic feature does enhance the emotion of the text. In addition, the effect of the model combining text with the image is similar to that of the model combining topic. But the model combining both modes improves more than the model with only one of them. If we use our method to fuse the three modalities, the overall performance of the model has been further improved. We can achieve an accuracy of 79.1% on average.

Table 3. Experimental results of ablation analysis on Weibo dataset.

Model	Precision	Recall	F1	Accuracy
CMHF + T	0.7156	0.7279	0.7156	0.7680
CMHF + P	0.6517	0.6365	0.6429	0.7100
CMHF + V	0.5647	0.5556	0.5595	0.6410
CMHF + TP	0.7275	0.7464	0.7358	0.7760
CMHF + TV	0.7369	0.7303	0.7329	0.7800
CMHF + PV	0.6538	0.6530	0.6531	0.7130
CMHF + TPV	0.7455	0.7445	0.7450	0.7820
CMHAF	**0.7542**	**0.7516**	**0.7514**	**0.7910**

Figure 6 shows the accuracy and F1 results of the model ablation experiment more intuitively. The performance of the model with two features is better than that of the single modal model which contains one of the two features. The accuracy of the models with text features are higher overall. On the other hand, the accuracy of any model is improved after integrating topic features. Moreover, the model with two cross-modal hierarchical attention fusion also improves performance.

These results of the ablation experiments once again prove the effectiveness of our method. More importantly, each part of the proposed model makes contributes to the performance of the whole model.

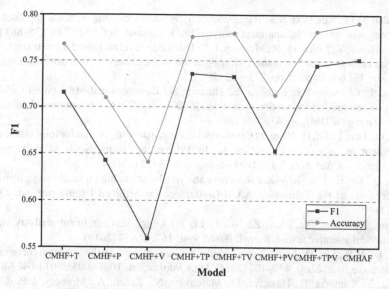

Fig. 6. Ablation analysis results on accuracy and F1.

5 Conclusion

In this paper, we introduce a multimodal sentiment analysis model CMHAF. The model extracts topic contents to capture cross-modal correlations. Furthermore, we present a cross-modal global fusion to combine the low-level visual features of the image and the sentence features of the text. A cross-modal high-level semantic fusion is introduced to combine the high-level semantic features of images and topic features. We evaluate the effectiveness of the proposed method on a real social media dataset. The experimental results show that our model outperforms the baseline model in several metrics and the extracted topic information successfully enhances the emotional semantics of the text modal. Similarly, the proposed fusion methods can effectively combine cross-modal features. The results also indicate that text modal contributes more to emotional expression than image modal in social media reviews.

In the future, we will continue to focus on the fusion strategy of multimodal features to enhance the performance of sentiment analysis. On the other hand, we also consider adding more modal information to improve the scalability of the model.

Acknowledgments. This work was supported by Hainan Provincial Natural Science Foundation of China (No. 620RC565) and National Natural Science Foundation of China (No. 61862021).

References

1. Tsai, Y.H.H., Liang, P.P., Zadeh, A., Morency, L.P., Salakhutdinov, R.: Learning factorized multimodal representations. In: International Conference on Learning Representations (2018)

2. Huddar, M.G., Sannakki, S.S., Rajpurohit, V.S.: A survey of computational approaches and challenges in multimodal sentiment analysis. Int. J. Comput. Sci. Eng. **7**(1), 876–883 (2019)
3. Pérez-Rosas, V., Mihalcea, R., Morency, L.P.: Utterance-level multimodal sentiment analysis. In: Proceedings of the 51st Annual Meeting of the Association for Computational Linguistics (Volume 1: Long Papers), pp. 973–982 (2013)
4. Poria, S., Chaturvedi, I., Cambria, E., Hussain, A.: Convolutional MKL based multimodal emotion recognition and sentiment analysis. In: 2016 IEEE 16th International Conference on Data Mining (ICDM), pp. 439–448 (2016)
5. You, Q., Luo, J., Jin, H., Yang, J.: Cross-modality consistent regression for joint visual-textual sentiment analysis of social multimedia. In: Proceedings of the Ninth ACM International Conference on Web Search and Data Mining, pp. 13–22 (2016)
6. You, Q., Jin, H., Luo, J.: Visual sentiment analysis by attending on local image regions. In: Proceedings of the Thirty-First AAAI Conference on Artificial Intelligence, pp. 231–237 (2017)
7. Huang, F., Zhang, X., Zhao, Z., Xu, J., Li, Z.: Image–text sentiment analysis via deep multimodal attentive fusion. Knowl.-Based Syst. **167**, 26–37 (2019)
8. Cao, D., Ji, R., Lin, D., Li, S.: A cross-media public sentiment analysis system for microblog. Multimedia Syst. **22**(4), 479–486 (2014). https://doi.org/10.1007/s00530-014-0407-8
9. Poria, S., Cambria, E., Hazarika, D., Majumder, N., Zadeh, A., Morency, L.P.: Context-dependent sentiment analysis in user-generated videos. In: Proceedings of the 55th Annual Meeting of the Association for Computational Linguistics, pp. 873–883 (2017)
10. Yadollahi, A., Shahraki, A.G., Zaiane, O.R.: Current state of text sentiment analysis from opinion to emotion mining. ACM Comput. Surv. (CSUR) **50**(2), 1–33 (2017)
11. Tang, D., Qin, B., Liu, T.: Document modeling with gated recurrent neural network for sentiment classification. In: Proceedings of the 2015 Conference on Empirical Methods in Natural Language Processing, pp. 1422–1432 (2015)
12. Siersdorfer, S., Minack, E., Deng, F., Hare, J.: Analyzing and predicting sentiment of images on the social web. In: Proceedings of the 18th ACM International Conference on Multimedia, pp. 715–718 (2010)
13. You, Q., Luo, J., Jin, H., Yang, J.: Robust image sentiment analysis using progressively trained and domain transferred deep networks. In: Proceedings of the Twenty-Ninth AAAI Conference on Artificial Intelligence, pp. 381–388 (2015)
14. Zadeh, A.B., Liang, P.P., Poria, S., Cambria, E., Morency, L.P.: Multimodal language analysis in the wild: CMU-MOSEI dataset and interpretable dynamic fusion graph. In: Proceedings of the 56th Annual Meeting of the Association for Computational Linguistics, pp. 2236–2246 (2018)
15. Zhang, X., Zhao, J., LeCun, Y.: Character-level convolutional networks for text classification. Adv. Neural. Inf. Process. Syst. **28**, 649–657 (2015)
16. Severyn, A., Moschitti, A.: Twitter sentiment analysis with deep convolutional neural networks. In: Proceedings of the 38th International ACM SIGIR Conference on Research and Development in Information Retrieval, pp. 959–962 (2015)
17. Irsoy, O., Cardie, C.: Deep recursive neural networks for compositionality in language. In: Advances in Neural Information Processing Systems, pp. 2096–2104 (2014)
18. Xiao, Z., Liang, P.: Chinese sentiment analysis using bidirectional LSTM with word embedding. In: International Conference on Cloud Computing and Security, pp. 601–610 (2016)
19. Xu, J., Chen, D., Qiu, X., Huang, X. J.: Cached long short-term memory neural networks for document-level sentiment classification. In: Proceedings of the 2016 Conference on Empirical Methods in Natural Language Processing, pp. 1660–1669 (2016)

20. Wang, J., Yu, L.C., Lai, K.R., Zhang, X.: Dimensional sentiment analysis using a regional CNN-LSTM model. In: Proceedings of the 54th Annual Meeting of the Association for Computational Linguistics, pp. 225–230 (2016)
21. Mnih, V., Heess, N., Graves, A.: Recurrent models of visual attention. In: Advances in neural information processing systems, pp. 2204–2212 (2014)
22. Bahdanau, D., Cho, K., Bengio, Y.: Neural machine translation by jointly learning to align and translate. arXiv preprint arXiv:1409.0473 (2014)
23. Vaswani, A., et al.: Attention is all you need. In: Advances in Neural Information Processing Systems, pp. 5998–6008 (2017)
24. Long, F., Zhou, K., Ou, W.: Sentiment analysis of text based on bidirectional LSTM with multi-head attention. IEEE Access 7, 141960–141969 (2019)
25. Peters, M.E., et al.: Deep contextualized word representations. arXiv preprint arXiv:1802. 05365 (2018)
26. Devlin, J., Chang, M.W., Lee, K., Toutanova, K.: Bert: Pre-training of deep bidirectional transformers for language understanding. arXiv preprint arXiv:1810.04805 (2018)
27. Brown, T.B., et al.: Language models are few-shot learners. arXiv preprint arXiv:2005.14165 (2020)
28. Yuan, J., Mcdonough, S., You, Q., Luo, J.: Sentribute: image sentiment analysis from a mid-level perspective. In: Proceedings of the Second International Workshop on Issues of Sentiment Discovery and Opinion Mining, pp. 1–8 (2013)
29. Borth, D., Ji, R., Chen, T., Breuel, T., Chang, S.F.: Large-scale visual sentiment ontology and detectors using adjective noun pairs. In: Proceedings of the 21st ACM International Conference on Multimedia, pp. 223–232 (2013)
30. Cao, D., Ji, R., Lin, D., Li, S.: Visual sentiment topic model based microblog image sentiment analysis. Multimedia Tools Appl. 75(15), 8955–8968 (2014). https://doi.org/10.1007/s11042-014-2337-z
31. Rao, T., Li, X., Xu, M.: Learning multi-level deep representations for image emotion classification. Neural Process. Lett. 51(3), 2043–2061 (2020)
32. Zhang, W., He, X., Lu, W.: Exploring discriminative representations for image emotion recognition with CNNs. IEEE T. Multimedia. 22(2), 515–523 (2019)
33. Simonyan, K., Zisserman, A.: Very deep convolutional networks for large-scale image recognition. arXiv preprint arXiv:1409.1556 (2014)
34. He, K., Zhang, X., Ren, S., Sun, J.: Deep residual learning for image recognition. In: Proceedings of the IEEE Conference on Computer Vision and Pattern Recognition, pp. 770–778 (2016)
35. Huang, G., Liu, Z., Van Der Maaten, L., Weinberger, K.Q.: Densely connected convolutional networks. In: Proceedings of the IEEE Conference on Computer Vision and Pattern Recognition, pp. 4700–4708 (2017)
36. Zhao, Z., et al.: An image-text consistency driven multimodal sentiment analysis approach for social media. Inf. Process. Manage. 56(6), 102097 (2019)
37. Guoyong, C., Guangrui, L., Zhi, X.: A hierarchical deep correlative fusion network for sentiment classification in social media. J. Res. Dev. 56(6), 1312 (2019)
38. Truong, Q.T., Lauw, H.W.: Vistanet: visual aspect attention network for multimodal sentiment analysis. In: Proceedings of the AAAI Conference on Artificial Intelligence, pp. 305–312 (2019)
39. Xu, N., Mao, W., Chen, G.: Multi-interactive memory network for aspect based multimodal sentiment analysis. In: Proceedings of the AAAI Conference on Artificial Intelligence, pp. 371–378 (2019)
40. Cai, Y., Cai, H., Wan, X.: Multi-modal sarcasm detection in twitter with hierarchical fusion model. In: Proceedings of the 57th Annual Meeting of the Association for Computational Linguistics, pp. 2506–2515 (2019)

41. Zadeh, A., Chen, M., Poria, S., Cambria, E., Morency, L.P.: Tensor fusion network for multi-modal sentiment analysis. In: Proceedings of the 2017 Conference on Empirical Methods in Natural Language Processing, pp. 1103–1114 (2017)
42. Guo, X., Ma, J., Zubiaga, A.: NUAA-QMUL at SemEval-2020 Task 8: Utilizing BERT and DenseNet for Internet Meme Emotion Analysis. arXiv preprint arXiv:2011.02788 (2020)

Application Track

Quantum Attention Based Language Model for Answer Selection

Qin Zhao[1], Chenguang Hou[2], and Ruifeng Xu[1(✉)]

[1] Harbin Institute of Technology, Shenzhen 518055, China
xuruifeng@hit.edu.cn
[2] Centre for Remote Imaging, Sensing and Processing,
National University of Singapore, 10 Lower Kent Ridge Road,
Blk S17, Level 2, Singapore 119076, Singapore

Abstract. Attention mechanism originally introduced for machine translation has a wide application in NLP tasks. By attending more important data with higher wight, the mechanism has the potential to improve neural networks' performance. Meanwhile, along with the pursuit of higher performance is the challenge of neural networks' interpretability. Based on quantum probability theory, quantum language model is just such an attempt and has drawn increasing attention. In this paper, we intend to investigate a balance between model's performance and interpretability, and propose a quantum attention based language model. Density matrix which carries the appearance probability of any word is used to construct quantum attention. Applied in a typical Question Answering task—Answer Selection, our model shows an effective performance on TREC-QA and WIKI-QA datasets.

Keywords: Attention mechanism · Quantum language model · Question answering · Answer selection

1 Introduction

Deep learning neural networks have achieved great success in a wide range of applications. One prevalent part in neural network pipelines is attention model, which is originally introduced for Machine Translation [1], has been widely applied in Natural Language Processing (NLP) [2,3], Speech [7], and Computer Vision [4]. By attending differently to different texts when constructing word and sentence representations, attention mechanism largely improves models' performance in NLP tasks. Modeling attention for machine translation, Bahdunau et al. [1] built a model with a better alignment of sentences in different languages. This alignment can help to capture subject-verb-noun locations. Yang et al. introduced attention model to document classification, specifically applied in word- and sentence- level [3]. Self attention is introduced to build more effective sentence or document representations. Wang et al. applied attention mechanism in sentiment analysis by utilizing attention to appropriately weight the concepts [5].

© Springer Nature Switzerland AG 2022
Y. Pan et al. (Eds.): AIMS 2021, LNCS 12987, pp. 47–57, 2022.
https://doi.org/10.1007/978-3-030-96033-9_4

Accompanied the endless pursuit of model's better performance is the challenge to increasing models' interpretability. A promising attempt is Quantum Language Model (QLM), which is based on quantum probability theory and tries to explain model in a deep view, having drawn increasing attention in NLP area [14,15]. As a generalization of traditional language models which utilize probabilistic models to measure the uncertainty of a text [12,13], QLMs show excellent interpretability and comparable performance to strong Convolutional Neural Network (CNN) [10] and Long Short-term Memory (LSTM) [11] baselines. Sordoni, Nie and Bengio [14] for the first time proposed a QLM, aiming to model the term dependency in a principled manner. A density matrix is introduced to represent a document and a query. Documents are ranked based on von-Neumann (vN) divergence between question and document density matrices. Applied to ad-hoc information retrieval task, QLM has achieved effective performance. Later, Zhang et al. proposed a Neural Network based Quantum-like Language Model (NNQLM) [16], which is an end-to-end trainable network, and applied it to Question Answering (QA) task. In order to find a better interpretability of neural network, Li et al. [17] built a Complex valued Network for Matching (CNM). Experiment results show that CNM has comparable performance with standard CNN and RNN baselines.

Inspired by the exciting progress in quantum-inspired language models and the significant achievement of the attention mechanism, we are interested to combine their advantages and construct a quantum attention based language model. Attention can be treated as a dynamic form of pooling to select different words with different probabilities to form the final document representation. Density matrix in a quantum system implies the appearance probability of any word. Therefore, it is reasonable to design a quantum attention using density matrix. In this paper, we propose a quantum attention based language model. Our model is applied to a typical QA task—Answer Selection, which aims to find the most appropriate answer from candidate answers for a question. To measure the model's performance, two benchmarking QA datasets are used, namely TREC-QA and WIKI-QA. Experiment results show that our proposed model is practically well-performed.

The rest of the paper is organized as follows. Section 2 presents a brief review of the related work on attention mechanism and quantum language models. Section 3 introduces some basic quantum terminology. In Sect. 4, we explain our constructed quantum attention based language model in detail. Section 5 shows our model's experimental results and discussion. Finally, we make a conclusion in Sect. 6.

2 Related Work

In this section, we briefly introduce the related work on attention mechanism and quantum language models.

2.1   Attention Mechanism

Attention mechanism originally introduced for Machine Translation [1] has become a prevalent part in neural network pipelines, which has been widely applied in NLP [2,3], Speech [7] and Computer Vision [4]. It is traditionally used as a feature extractor. Galassi et al. proposed a taxonomy of attention models according to the representation of input, compatibility function, distribution function and multiplicity of the input and output [2]. Xu et al. introduced a two attention based model that automatically learns to describe the content of images [8]. Anderson et al. proposed a combined bottom-up and top-down attention mechanism that enables attention to be calculated at the level of objects and other salient image regions [9].

In NLP domain, attention can attend different words or texts with different weight, align sequences in a better way, capture long range dependencies for longer sequences. Bahdunau et al. [1] introduced attention mechanism to machine translation and obtained a better alignment of sentences in different languages. Attention used in question answering helps the model to better understand question, and further improves a model's performance [6]. Yang et al. [3] made use of self attention to build more effective sentence and document representation. A hierarchical attention structure captures word- and sentence-level representations with different weight. Experiments conducted intensively demonstrate their model's effectiveness.

2.2   Quantum Inspired Models

Van Rijsbergen (2004) originally proposed to exploit the mathematical formalism of quantum theory to the logical geometric, and probalistic IR models [19]. Inspired by this seeming work, a range of work based on the analogy between quantum phenomena and natural language processing tasks has been done [20–23]. According to the analogy between IR ranking and quantum interference phenomena, Zuccon et al. proposed a quantum probability ranking principle [21]. Zhao et al. utilized a filtering process in photon polarization to construct a quantum-inspired ranking method [22].

Sordoni, Nie and Bengio [14] for the first time came up with a QLM, for which the density matrix is important. This model can be treated as a generalization of traditional language models. Later, using the idea of quantum entropy minimization, Sordoni et al. proposed a supervised way to learn latent concept embeddings for query expansion [24]. To describe the dynamic information need in search session, Li et al. [25] constructed an adaptive QLM with an evolution process of density matrix.

Later, quantum language models have been broadened from IR to QA tasks. Zhang et al. [16] proposed an end-to-end quantum-like language model. A density matrix is built to represent a sentence. Li et al. [17] proposed a complex-valued network by considering the analogy between complex-valued physical state and word in QLM. Zhao et al. [18] constructed a quantum expectation value based language model by introducing quantum observable.

3   Basic Concepts

Quantum probability theory [26,27], a generalization of the classical one, has a special mathematical formalism for interpreting in quantum phenomena. The probabilistic space is a vector space, named Hilbert space, denoted as $\mathbb{H}^n$. We use Dirac notation to represent a unit vector in this space. A unit vector $\mathbf{u} \in \mathbb{H}$ and its transpose $\mathbf{u}^T$ are written as a *ket* $|u\rangle$ and a *bra* $\langle u|$, respectively. An event Π written as $|u\rangle\langle u|$, is a projection operator on a subspace, which also is called as a *dyad*. An inner product between two state vectors $|u\rangle$ and $|v\rangle$ is represented as $\langle u|v\rangle$. Given an orthonormal bases $\{|e_i\rangle\}_{i=1}^n$ for $\mathbb{H}^n$, an arbitrary vector $|u\rangle$ can be expanded as follows:

$$|u\rangle = \sum_{i=1}^n u_i|e_i\rangle, \tag{1}$$

where u_i is the probability amplitude along $|e_i\rangle$ and $\sum_i u_i^2 = 1$.

Density matrices are a generalization of the classical finite probability distributions in quantum probability theory, which is a symmetric, positive semi-definite matrix with trace being one. A density matrix can be written as a mixture over dyads,

$$\rho = \sum_i p_i|\psi_i\rangle\langle\psi_i|, \tag{2}$$

where $\{|\psi_i\rangle\}_{i=1}^n$ are pure states and $p_i \geq 0$ is the corresponding probability.

To find out the probability of a particular state $|u\rangle$, one can use Gleason's theorem [28,29] through projection operator $|u\rangle\langle u|$,

$$\mu_\rho(|u\rangle\langle u|) = \text{tr}(\rho|u\rangle\langle u|), \tag{3}$$

where tr is a trace operator. This measure μ ensures that $\mu(|u\rangle\langle u||\rho) \geq 0$.

4   Quantum Attention Based Language Model

In quantum language model, quantum system's Hilbert space $\mathbb{H}^n$ is the semantic space. It is spanned by a set of orthogonal basis states $\{|e_j\rangle\}_{j=1}^n$, with $|e_j\rangle$ being a sememe representing a semantic unit [30]. A unit state $\{|e_j\rangle\}$ is a one-hot vector. That is, except the j-th element in $\{|e_j\rangle\}$ is one, other elements are all zero. Our proposed Quantum Attention based Language Model (QALM) is root from this background. It consists of a word encoder, quantum probability based attention and sentence representation, sentence feature selection and matching. The sketch of the model is shown in Fig. 1, whose detailed components are explained as follows.

4.1   Word Encoder

A word w is treated as a superposition of sememes $\{|e_j\rangle\}_{j=1}^n$, with the value vector being its word embedding obtained from a word embedding lookup table. To obtain a unit state vector, a L2 normalization is operated as follows:

$$|w\rangle = \frac{\mathbf{w}}{\| \mathbf{w} \|}, \tag{4}$$

where $\| \mathbf{w} \|$ denotes L2-norm of $\mathbf{w}$.

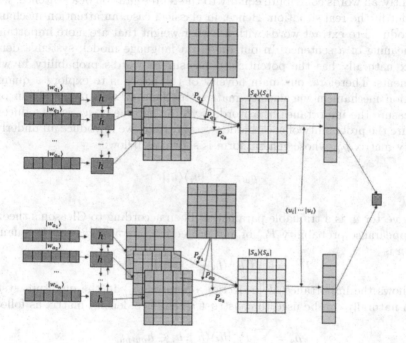

Fig. 1. The sketch of quantum attention based language model (QALM).

As context information can play a important role in word's representation, we utilize a bidirectional long short term memory network piped after work encoding. Given a sentence $\{w_t\}_{t=1}^n$, we get:

$$\overrightarrow{h_t} = \overrightarrow{LSTM}(w_t), t \in [1, n]. \tag{5}$$

$$\overleftarrow{h_t} = \overleftarrow{LSTM}(w_t), t \in [1, n]. \tag{6}$$

$$h_{output} = \frac{\overrightarrow{h_t} + \overleftarrow{h_t}}{2}. \tag{7}$$

Here, $\overrightarrow{h_t}$ denotes the output of the forward-directional LSTM, and $\overleftarrow{h_t}$ denotes the output of the opposite-directional LSTM. In order to combine both directions' information and meanwhile keep hidden states' dimension, we construct the output hidden state as the element-wise average of $\overrightarrow{h_t}$ and $\overleftarrow{h_t}$. Therefore, each hidden state contains the information from context. After we obtain hidden states' representations, we can construct the corresponding projection operators:

$$\Pi_{h_i} = |h_i\rangle\langle h_i|, h_i \in h_{output}. \tag{8}$$

4.2 Quantum Attention and Sentence Representation

Currently, all words contribute equally to the representation of a sentence, which does not fit the real situation. Hence, in classical case, an attention mechanism is introduced to extract words with a higher weight that are more important to the meaning of a sentence. In our quantum language model, system's density matrix naturally has the potential to measure a word's probability in whole documents. Therefore, our main novelty of the paper is to explore a quantum attention mechanism via density matrix. In Yang et al.'s paper [3], in order to measure the importance of a word, a vector parameter u_w is introduced to measure the probability of each hidden vector. Here, we introduce an underlying density matrix ρ_u, whose general form is shown as below:

$$\rho_u = \sum_i |u_i\rangle\langle u_i|. \tag{9}$$

where vector u_i is a trainable parameter. Then according to Gleason's theorem, the appearance probability P_{h_i} of any projection operator $|h_i\rangle$ in the quantum system is

$$P_{h_i} = \mu_{\rho_u}(|h_i\rangle\langle h_i|) = \mathrm{tr}(\rho_u|h_i\rangle\langle h_i|). \tag{10}$$

P_{h_i} shows the importance of projection operator $|h_i\rangle$ in the quantum system, which naturally can be used to construct a sentence density matrix as follows:

$$\rho_s = \sum_i P_{h_i}|h_i\rangle\langle h_i|, h_i \in h_{output}. \tag{11}$$

Therefore, a sentence which contains an assemble of words, can correspond to a mixed state represented by a density matrix.

4.3 Sentence feature selection and Matching

After sentence density matrix is constructed, we introduce a series of trainable vectors $\{|\lambda_k\rangle\}_{k=1}^{K}$ to extract density matrix features. For a sentence density matrix, these vectors can produce a k dimensional vector, $[P_{\lambda_1}, P_{\lambda_2}, \cdots, P_{\lambda_K}]$. The i-th element P_{λ_i} in this vector shows the appearance probability of vector $|\lambda_i\rangle$ under that sentence density matrix. We treat such k dimensional vector as the corresponding sentence feature representations. For a question sentence and its corresponding answer sentence, we do the same operation and then obtain both feature representations. A cosine similarity between question and answer feature representations is used to measure the matching score of the question-answer pairs, denoted as $Score_{qa}$. Negative cross entropy loss is used to train the model.

$$\mathcal{L} = -\sum_{i}^{N}[y_i\log(Score_{qa}) + (1 - y_i)\log(1 - Score_{qa})]. \qquad (12)$$

5 Experiment

5.1 Experimental Setup

The experiments are conducted on two standard benchmarking QA datasets which are summarized in Table 1.

Table 1. Statistics of TREC-QA and WIKI-QA datasets.

Dataset	Question			Pairs		
	train	dev	test	train	dev	test
TREC-QA	1229	65	68	53417	117	1442
WIKI-QA	837	126	633	8627	1130	2351

- TREC-QA [31]: a standard QA dataset in the Text REtrieval Conference (TREC).
- WIKI-QA [32]: an open domain QA dataset released by Microsoft Research.

The task on both datasets aims to choose the most suitable answer from multiple candidate answers for a question. Before the training process, data cleaning process is done by removing the questions with no correct answers. This can make sure every question has at least one correct answer. The evaluation metrics are two commonly used ones for the same task with the same datasets, that is, Mean Average Precision (MAP) and Mean Reciprocal Rank (MRR).

5.2 Baselines

The baselines for comparison include a wide range of quantum language models, since our mode is a quantum-like attention model. They are,

- **QLM** [14]. Density matrices ρ_q and ρ_a for question and answer sentences are constructed respectively, with diagonal elements being term frequency values of the corresponding words. von-Neumann divergence between ρ_q and ρ_a is adopted to measure the matching score of question-answer pairs.

- **NNQLM-II** [16]. It is an end-to-end quantum language model. Embedding vector encoded as word state representation is used to build sentence density matrix. The matching score is calculated based on joint representation of question-answer density matrices.
- **CNM** [17]. Words are treated as a complex physical states in the quantum system, and hence they are encoded with complex-valued embedding. Projectors are introduced to select density matrix's features. Cosine similarity between question and answer sentences' features is the matching score.

Besides the quantum language model, we also choose a set of traditional language models as our baselines. They are Ngram-CNN [33,34], Multi-Perspective CNN (MP-CNN) [35] and three-layer stacked bidirectional Long Short-term Memory with BM25 (Three-Layer BiLSTM with BM25) [36], Long Short-term Memory with attention (LSTM-attn) [37].

5.3   Experiment Settings

The trainable parameters are the word embedding values, LSTM hidden states, attention density matrix and the projection vectors used to select sentence feature representations. We first initialize word vectors with 50-dimension Glove vectors and perform L2 regularization to normalize it to unite length. Adam optimizer with learning rate among $[1e-5, 5e-4, 1e-3, 1e-2]$ is adopted, and the batch size is tuned around $[16,32]$. We train our model for 100 epochs and choose the best model obtained in the dev data set to evaluate the test dataset.

5.4   Experimental Results and Discussion

Table 2 shows the experiment results on TREC-QA and WIKI-QA datasets, where the best values are shown in bold. Our model achieves comparable results with other quantum-inspired language models. Especially, it has performed best on 3 metrics on TREC-QA and WIKI-QA. This demonstrates the effectiveness of our proposed model. On TREC-QA and WIKI-QA dataset, QALM significantly outperforms QLM and NNQLM-II. Specifically, on TREC-QA dataset, QALM surpasses QLM by 15.60% on MAP and 19.16% on MRR, respectively; QALM performs better than NNQLM-II by 3.33% on MAP and 4.92% on MRR, respectively. On WIKI-QA dataset, QALM outperforms QLM by 30.85% on MAP and 34.16% on MRR, respectively; QALM performs better than NNQLM-II by 2.90% on MAP and 4.76% on MRR, respectively. QALM also has comparable performance with CNM. Especially, it performs better on TREC-QA dataset. Compared with standard CNN and RNN models, QALM dramatically outperforms Ngram-CNN, and also achieves better performance than other baselines.

Table 2. Experimental results on TREC-QA and WIKIQA datasets. The best performed values are in bold.

Model	TREC-QA		WIKIQA	
	MAP	MRR	MAP	MRR
Ngram-CNN	0.6709	0.7280	0.6661	0.6851
MP-CNN	0.7770	0.8360	/	/
Three-Layer BiLSTM with BM25	0.7134	0.7913	/	/
LSTM-attn	/	/	0.6639	0.6828
QLM	0.6784	0.7265	0.5109	0.5148
NNQLM-II	0.7589	0.8254	0.6496	0.6594
CNM	0.7701	0.8591	**0.6748**	0.6864
QALM	**0.7842**	**0.8660**	0.6685	**0.6908**

Table 3 shows the ablation analysis. Here we mainly consider two ablation experiments. QALM-no-atten is a model without attention mechanism. Sentence density matrix is an equal contribution of all words' density matrix. On both TREC-QA and WIKI-QA dataset, Table 3 shows that QALM-no-atten performs worse than QALM. QALM-no-density is a model where sentence representation only considers sentence density matrix' diagonal terms. Therefore, sentence representation is degenerated to the common one in classical model. Compared with QALM, QALM-no-density also has a worse performance. The ablation studies demonstrate the effectiveness of introducing quantum attention in our model.

Table 3. Ablation analysis.

Model	TREC-QA		WIKIQA	
	MAP	MRR	MAP	MRR
QALM-no-atten	0.7550	0.8212	0.6369	0.6398
QALM-no-density	0.7641	0.8504	0.6601	0.6804
QALM	0.7842	0.8660	0.6685	0.6908

6   Conclusion

In this paper, we propose a Quantum Attention based Language Model. We investigate a combination of classical attention mechanism and quantum language model. Using density matrix to construct quantum attention, we can construct a more powerful sentence representation. Experiment results on TREC-QA and WIKI-QA datasets show that our proposed model is practically well-performed.

Acknowledgments. This work was partially supported by National Natural Science Foundation of China 62006062, 61876053, Shenzhen Foundational Research Funding JCYJ2018 0507183527919, China Postdoctoral Science Foundation 2020M670912.

References

1. Bahdanau, D., Cho, K., Bengio, Y.: Neural machine translation by jointly learning to align and translate. arXiv preprint, arXiv:1409.0473 (2014)
2. Galassi, A., Lippi, M., Torroni, P.: Attention in natural language processing. IEEE Trans. Neural Netw. Learn. Syst. **32**(10), 4291–4308 (2021)
3. Yang, Z., Yang, D., Dyer, C., He, X., Smola, A., Hovy, E.: Hierarchical attention networks for document classification. In: Proceedings of the 2016 Conference of the North American Chapter of the Association for Computational Linguistics: Human Language Technologies, pp. 1480–1489 (2016)
4. Wang, F., Tax, M.J.D.: Survey on the attention based RNN model and its applications in computer vision. arXiv preprint, arXiv:1601.06823 (2016)
5. Wang, Y., Huang, M., Zhu, X., Zhao, L.: Attention-based LSTM for aspect-level sentiment classification. In: Proceedings of the 2016 Conference on Empirical Methods in Natural Language Processing. Association for Computational Linguistics, pp. 606–615 (2016)
6. Hermann, K.M., et al.: Teaching machines to read and comprehend. Adv. Neural Inf. Process. Syst. **28**, 1693–1701. Curran Associates Inc. (2015)
7. Cho, K., Courville, A., Bengio, Y.: Describing multimedia content using attention-based encoder- decoder networks. IEEE Trans. Multimed. **17**(11), 1875–1886 (2015)
8. Xu, K., et al.: Show, attend and tell: neural image caption generation with visual attention. In: Proceeding of ICML, pp. 2048–2057 (2015)
9. Anderson, P., et al.: Bottom-up and top-down attention for image captioning and visual question answering. In: Proceeding of CVPR, pp. 6077–6086 (2018)
10. Yu, L., Moritz Hermann, K., Blunsom, P., Pulman, S.: Deep learning for answer sentence selection. arXiv preprint, arXiv:1412.1632 (2014)
11. Dos Santos, C., Tan, M., Xiang, B., Zhou, B.: Attentive pooling networks. arXiv preprint, arXiv:1602.03609 (2016)
12. Melucci, M., Van Rijsbergen, K.: Quantum Mechanics and Information Retrieval, pp. 125–155. Springer, Berlin, Heidelberg (2011)
13. Sordoni, A., Nie, J.-Y.: Looking at vector space and language models for IR using density matrices. In: Atmanspacher, H., Haven, E., Kitto, K., Raine, D. (eds.) QI 2013. LNCS, vol. 8369, pp. 147–159. Springer, Heidelberg (2014). https://doi.org/10.1007/978-3-642-54943-4_13
14. Sordoni, A., Nie, J., Bengio, Y.: Modeling term dependencies with quantum language models for IR. In: Proceeding of Special Interest Group on Information Retrieval, pp. 653–662. ACM (2013)
15. Levine, Y., Yakira, D., Cohen, N., Shashua, A.: Deep learning and quantum entanglement: Fundamental connections with implications to network design. arXiv:1704.01552 (2017)
16. Zhang, P., Niu, J., Su, Z., Wang, B., Ma, L., Song, D.: End-to-end quantum-like language models with application to question answering. In: Proceeding of Association for the Advancement of Artificial Intelligence, pp. 5666–5673 (2018)
17. Li, Q., Wang, B., Melucci, M.: CNM: an interpretable complex-valued network for matching. In: Proceeding of North American Chapter of the Association for Computational Linguistics, pp. 4139–4148 (2019)
18. Zhao, Q., Hou, C., Liu, C., Zhang, P., Xu, R.: A quantum expectation value based language model with application to question answering. Entropy **22**, 533 (2020)

19. Van Rijsbergen, C.J.: The Geometry of Information Retrieval. Cambridge University Press, Cambridge (2004)
20. Piwowarski, B., Frommholz, I., Lalmas, M., van Rijsbergen, K.: What can quantum theory bring to information retrieval. In: Proceeding of Conference on Information and Knowledge Management, pp. 59–68 (2010)
21. Zuccon, G., Azzopardi, L.: Using the quantum probability ranking principle to rank interdependent documents. In: Proceeding of European Conference on Information Retrieval, pp. 357–369 (2010)
22. Zhao, X., Zhang, P., Song, D., Hou, Y.: A novel reranking approach inspired by quantum measurement. In: Proceeding of European Conference on Information Retrieval, pp. 721–724 (2011)
23. Zhang, P., et al.: A quantum query expansion approach for session search. Entropy 18(4), 146 (2016)
24. Sordoni, A., Bengio, Y., Nie, J.: Learning concept embeddings for query expansion by quantum entropy minimization. In: Proceeding of Association for the Advancement of Artificial Intelligence, vol. 14, pp. 1586–1592 (2014)
25. Li, Q., Li, J., Zhang, P., Song, D.: Modeling multi-query retrieval tasks using density matrix transformation. In: Proceeding of Special Interest Group on Information Retrieval, pp. 871–874. ACM (2015)
26. Neumann, V.: Mathematical Foundations of Quantum Mechanics. Number 2. Princeton University Press, Princeton (1955)
27. Nielsen, M.A., Chuang, I.L.: Quantum Computation and Quantum Information. Cambridge University Press, Cambridge, New York (2010)
28. Gleason, A.M.: Measures on the closed subspaces of a hilbert space. J. Appl. Math. Mech. 885–893 (1957)
29. Hughes, R.I.: The Structure and Interpretation of Quantum Mechanics. Harvard University Press, Cambridge (1992)
30. Goddard, C., Wierzbicka, A.: Semantic and Lexical Universals: Theory and Empirical Findings. John Benjamins Publishing, Amsterdam (1994)
31. Voorhees, E.M., Tice, D.M.: Building a question answering test collection. In: Proceeding of Special Interest Group on Information Retrieval, pp. 200–207 (2000)
32. Yang, Y., Yih, W., Meek, C.: WikiQA: a Challenge dataset for open-Domain question answering. In: Proceeding of Empirical Methods in Natural Language Processing, pp. 2013–2018. Association for Computational Linguistics (2015)
33. Severyn, A., Moschitti, A.: Learning to rank short text pairs with convolutional deep neural networks. In: Proceeding of Special Interest Group on Information Retrieval, pp. 373–382. ACM (2015)
34. Severyn, A., Moschitti, A.: Modeling relational information in question-answer pairs with convolutional neural networks. arXiv:1604.01178 (2016)
35. He, H., Gimpel, K., Lin, J.: MultiPerspective sentence similarity modeling with convolutional neural networks. In: Proceeding of Empirical Methods in Natural Language Processing, pp. 1576–1586. ACL (2015)
36. Wang, D., Nyberg, E.: A long short-term memory model for answer sentence selection in question answering. In: Proceeding of Association for Computational Linguistics, pp. 707–712 (2015)
37. Miao, Y., Yu, L., Blunsom, P.: Neural variational inference for text processing. arXiv:1511.06038 (2015)

LightBERT: A Distilled Chinese BERT Model

Yice Zhang[1], Yihui Li[1], Peng Xu[1], Ruifeng Xu[1(✉)], Jianxin Li[2],
Guozhong Shi[2], and Feiran Hu[2]

[1] Joint Lab of HITSZ-CMS, Harbin Institute of Technology (Shenzhen),
Shenzhen, China
{20s051013,19s051059}@stu.hit.edu.cn, xuruifeng@hit.edu.cn
[2] China Merchants Securities Co., Ltd., Shenzhen, China
{lijx,shiguozhong,hufeiran}@cmschina.com.cn

Abstract. Pre-trained language models (e.g. BERT) have achieve
remarkable performance in most natural language understanding tasks.
However, it's difficult to apply these models to online systems for their
huge amount of parameters and long inference time. Knowledge Distillation is a popular model compression technique, which could achieve considerable model structure compression with limited performance degradation. However, there are currently no knowledge distillation methods
specially designed for compressing Chinese pre-trained language model
and no corresponding distilled model has been publicly released. In this
paper, we propose LightBERT, which is a distilled Bert model specially
for Chinese Language Processing. We perform pre-training distillation
under the masking language model objective with whole word masking,
which is a masking strategy adapted to Chinese language characteristics.
Furthermore, we adopt a multi-step distillation strategy to compress the
model progressively. Experiments on CLUE benchmark show LightBERT
could reduce 62.5% size of a RoBERTa model while achieving 94.5% the
performance of its teacher.

Keywords: Model compression · Knowledge distillation · Language
model

1 Introduction

Transformer [18] demonstrates its excellent capabilities in sequence modeling
[10,20,21], and allows for significantly more parallelization. For these reasons,
transformer is widely applied to various pre-trained language models (PTMs),
represented by BERT [3]. After unsupervised pre-training on large-scale text corpus, PTMs exhibit potential language understanding, and could produce mean-
ingful contextual representations. Benefiting from these, PTMs greatly improve
the performance of various tasks in natural language understanding [3,9,11].
However, PLMs typically have large-scale parameters, which leads to considerable memory consumption and computation, and consequently significantly

© Springer Nature Switzerland AG 2022
Y. Pan et al. (Eds.): AIMS 2021, LNCS 12987, pp. 58–67, 2022.
https://doi.org/10.1007/978-3-030-96033-9_5

increases hardware requirement for its application in online systems. Meanwhile, some recent work [7,12,19] has shown there is redundancy in PTMs. To sum up, it is necessary and feasible to perform model compression while retaining their performances.

There are various model compression routes, and one major branch is knowledge distillation [4]. Knowledge distillation follows the teacher-student framework, where the teacher is a relatively large network and is trained-completed on a specific task. The student is trained to achieve its imitation of the teacher under the supervision of the teacher's logits and intermediate representations. Several works [6,15–17] have applied knowledge distillation to the compression of pre-trained language models. Sanh et al. [15] pioneers the application of knowledge distillation to BERT model compression, and proposed DistilBERT. They employ a reduced-layer BERT as the student and then train it through three objectives: *distillation* loss, *masked language modeling* loss and *cosine embedding* loss. Sanh et al. found that aligning student's feature representations with the teacher contributes to the knowledge transfer. Subsequently, Sun et al. [16] further introduces Patient Knowledge Distillation, in which the student learns from intermediate representations of the teacher for incremental knowledge transfer. Later, Jiao et al. [6] formally proposes a two-stage framework, which performs distillation at both the pre-training and task-specific learning stages. With the two-stage distillation and intermediate representations' supervision, current knowledge distillation technique could reduce the size of PTMs by a large margin, while retaining most of their language understanding capabilities. However, these knowledge distillation techniques are all designed for English Language Processing and no any Chinese distilled Bert model has been publicly released.

This paper proposes LightBERT, which is a distilled BERT model specially for Chinese Language Processing. We follow the two-stage distillation framework [6], which consists of pre-training distillation and fine-tuning distillation. In the pre-training distillation stage, the student model, i.e., a reduced-layer BERT model, is trained with mask language modeling objective and distillation objectives. Specifically, we adopt whole word masking (WWM) [2], a mask strategy specifically developed for Chinese language, for language masking. Furthermore, it has been demonstrated that knowledge transfer is difficult and inefficient when the size gap between teacher and student is too large [13]. To bridge this gap, we leverage a multi-step distillation strategy to compress the BERT model progressively. Concretely, one or more teaching assistants of model size between the teacher and the student are introduced to reduce the difficulty of knowledge transfer. We conduct experiments on CLUE benchmark, and results show LightBERT-3 could reduce 62.5% size of a RoBERTa model while achieving 94.5% the performance of its teacher. Besides, we also show that LightBERT-6 can achieve comparable performance with the teacher.

2   Preliminaries

2.1   Transformer Layer

Transformer [18] is a self-attention based network architecture, and therefore, let's first recap the self-attention operation.

The self-attention operation could be formalized as follows:

$$\text{attention}(Q,K,V) = \text{softmax}(\frac{QK^\top}{\sqrt{d_k}})V, \tag{1}$$

$$\text{self-attention}(H;W_Q,W_K,W_V) = \text{attention}(W_Q^\top H, W_K^\top H, W_V^\top H), \tag{2}$$

where W_Q, W_K, W_V are trainable parameters. In self-attention operation, the output hidden states at each time step is a weighted sum over input vectors $H = [\mathbf{h}_1, \cdots, \mathbf{h}_n]$, which allows representations at different time steps to interact directly with each other. Therefore, self-attention operation could capture long-distance dependencies more easily than LSTM [5]. More importantly, self-attention allows for better parallelism. Consequently, self-attention has been widely employed in various tasks of natural language processing.

Specifically, a standard transformer layer is composed of two sub-layers: *multi-head attention* and *feed-forward* network. Formally, a transformer layer could be defined as:

$$\text{Transformer}(H) = \text{FFN}(\text{MHA}(H)). \tag{3}$$

Multi-head Attention *allows the model to jointly attend to information from different representation subspaces at different positions* [18]. More specifically, in multi-head attention, self-attention operation is repeated several times, and then the outputs are concatenated and fed into a linear projection layer.

$$\text{multi-head-attention}(H) = W_O^\top[\text{head}_1; \cdots ; \text{head}_k], \tag{4}$$
$$\text{where } \text{head}_i = \text{self-attention}(H;W_{Qi}, W_{Ki}, W_{Vi}).$$

where $W_O, W_{Qi}, W_{Ki}, W_{Vi}$ are trainable parameters, k is the number of attention heads. Additionally, a residual connection is included to alleviate the network degradation issue in deep neural network.

$$\text{MHA}(H) = \text{LayerNorm}(\text{multi-head-attention}(H) + H). \tag{5}$$

Feed-forward Network increases the non-linearity of transformers, consisting of two linear transformation and one residual connection.

$$\text{FFN}(H) = \text{LayerNorm}(W_2^\top f(W_1^\top H) + H), \tag{6}$$

where W_1, W_2 are trainable parameters, $f(\cdot)$ is the activation function, and LayerNorm refers to the layer normalization operation [1].

2.2 Knowledge Distillation

Knowledge distillation is a knowledge transfer method proposed by hinton et al. [4]. It follows the teacher-student framework and allows knowledge to transfer from a original large teacher to a rather small student model. Let z^t and z^s be the logits outputs by the teacher and the student, then the distillation loss is

$$p^s = \text{softmax}(z^s/T), \tag{7}$$
$$p^t = \text{softmax}(z^t/T), \tag{8}$$
$$\mathcal{L}_{KD} = T^2 \times \text{KL}(p^t||p^s), \tag{9}$$

where T denotes the temperature, which is generally a larger number that smooths out the probability distribution, and KL denotes Kullback-Leibler Divergence [8]. Then, the student are optimized by minimizing $\mathcal{L}$.

$$\mathcal{L}_{CE} = \text{CE}(z^s, y), \tag{10}$$
$$\mathcal{L} = \alpha\mathcal{L}_{CE} + (1-\alpha)\mathcal{L}_{KD}, \tag{11}$$

where α is a hyperparameter.

Furthermore, subsequent researchers [14,16] employ the feature representation the teacher outputs as a supervision of the distillation process, which is experimentally demonstrated to be effective. Let H^t and H^s be the feature representations output by the teacher and the student, then the representation loss is

$$\text{rep-loss}(H^s, H^t) = \text{MSE}(H^s, H^t). \tag{12}$$

If their dimensions do not match, then a linear projection is applied.

$$\text{rep-loss}(H^s, H^t) = \text{MSE}(W^\top H^s, H^t), \tag{13}$$

where the transformation matrix W is a learnable parameter and is usually shared between different layers. Note that the hidden loss could not only be calculated on the final feature representation, but also embedding and intermediate representations.

3 Methodology

3.1 Student Architecture

Compared with the teacher model, i.e. the BERT model, the student model is generally a relatively small network. Besides, it has been shown that a good initialization can greatly accelerate the convergence of the student model [15].

The most straightforward approach is to utilize a reduced layer BERT model as the student model, as shown in the Fig. 1, and initialize it with every K layer of teacher model, where K is the ratio of the number of teacher layers to the number of student layers. Under this setting, every layer in the student model is expected to achieve the effect of K layers in the teacher model.

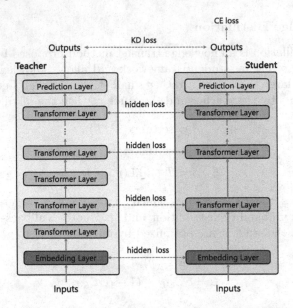

Fig. 1. Model architecture of LightBERT.

Apart from the network depth, we can also reduce the network width, for example, reducing the hidden size from 768 to 384. Under this setting, the student model's initialization could be implemented by loading weights from first 6 attention heads.

3.2   Pre-training Distillation

Pre-training stage distillation aims to transfer knowledge from the teacher to the student through the large-scale general text corpus. We follow the idea of Sanh et al. [15], where the teacher and the student are run on the masked language modeling task, and then distillation loss is calculated on the output of both. Differently, we adopt whole word masking strategy [2], where tokens in the same word are either masked together or not masked together. This strategy can be illustrated by Fig. 2.

After obtaining the teacher and student outputs, the student will be optimized by minimizing the following loss:

$$\mathcal{L} = (1 - \alpha_1)\mathcal{L}_{\text{CE}} + \alpha_1 \mathcal{L}_{\text{KD}} + \alpha_2 \mathcal{L}_{\text{hidden}}. \tag{14}$$

where α_1, α_2 are two hyperparameters, and $\mathcal{L}_{\text{hidden}}$ are calculated by:

$$\mathcal{L}_{\text{hidden}} = \frac{1}{n_{\text{slayer}} + 1} \sum_{l=0}^{n_{\text{slayer}}} \mathcal{L}_{\text{hidden}(l)}, \tag{15}$$

$$\mathcal{L}_{\text{hidden}(l)} = \text{rep-loss}(H^{s(l)}, H^{t(K \times l)}), \tag{16}$$

$$K = n_{\text{tlayer}}/n_{\text{slayer}}. \tag{17}$$

where $n_{\text{slayer}}(n_{\text{tlayer}})$ denotes the number of transformer layers in the student (teacher); $H^{s(l)}(H^{s(l)})$ are the lth layer's hidden states of the student (teacher), and $H^{s(0)}, H^{t(0)}$ represents the embedding of the input text.

[Original Sentence]

邓布利多是哈利波特中的一个角色

[Original Sentence with CWS]

邓布利多 是 哈利波特 中 一个 的 角色

[Original Masking Input]

邓布[MASK][MASK] 是 哈[MASK]波特 [MASK] 一个 的 角色

[Whole Word Masking Input]

[MASK][MASK][MASK][MASK] 是 哈利波特 [MASK] 一个 的 角色

Fig. 2. Example of the whole word masking strategy in BERT. CWS refers to Chinese Word Segmentation.

3.3 Multi-step Distillation

When the parameter size of the student is rather small, e.g. 3-layer transformer with 384 hidden size, the knowledge transfer from the teacher to the student will be inefficient for the big parameter size gap. Therefore, we follow Mirzadeh et al. [13], introducing the teacher assistant to bridge this gap. The teacher assistant is a network with medium parameter size. Knowledge from the teacher are first transferred to the teacher assistant, and then the student learns from the teacher assistant.

4 Experiment

4.1 Datasets

We evaluate LightBERT on the Chinese General Language Understanding Evaluation (CLUE) benchmark [22]. Note that only text classification tasks are used, and results on development set are reported. The data statistics and evaluation metrics are detailed in Table 1.

4.2 Implementation Details

The teacher model we used is RoBERTa-wwm-ext-base [2], hereafter referred to as RoBERTa-wwm, which contains 12 transformer layers with hidden size of 768. We adopt Chinese Wikipedia[1] and News Corpus [22] as the text corpora for pre-training distillation. We train the student model for 150K steps with a maximum sequence length of 128, batch size of 256. Initial learning rate is set

---

[1] https://dumps.wikimedia.org/zhwiki/latest/zhwiki-latest-pages-articles.xml.bz2.

Table 1. Task descriptions and statistics in CLUE.

Corpus	#Train	#Dev	#Test	Task	#class	Metric
Single-sentence tasks						
TNEWS	53.3k	10k	10k	Short text classification	15	Acc.
IFLYTEK	12.1k	2.6k	2.6k	Long text classification	119	Acc.
CLUEWSC2020	1,244	304	290	Coreference resolution	2	Acc.
Sentence pair tasks						
AFQMC	34.3k	4.3k	3.9k	Semantic similarity	2	Acc.
CSL	20k	3k	3k	Keyword recognition	2	Acc.
OCNLI	50k	3k	3k	Natural language inference	3	Acc.

according to the size of the student model, which is detailed in Table 2. We adopt `linear_scheduler` with warmup step of 1K to adjust the learning rate. Besides, we set hyperparameter $\alpha_1 = 0.7, \alpha_2 = 10, T = 10$. After pre-training distillation, we perform fine-tuning distillation with same hyperparameter setting.

Table 2. Setting for learning rate. L-6_H-768 represents a student model which contains 6 transformer layers with hidden size of 768.

Model	L-6_H-768	L-3_H-768	L-12_H-384	L-6_H-384	L-3_H-384
LR	6e−5	9e−5	10e−5	20e−5	30e−5

4.3   Baselines

We compare LightBERT with RoBERTa-3(6), RBT3[2] and PKD-BERT [16].

- Roberta-3(6) contains 3(6) transformer layers with hidden size of 768, which is directly initialized from Roberta-wwm.
- RBT3 has the same architecture as Roberta-3, and continue pre-training for 1M steps.
- PKD-BERT learns from the teacher's intermediate representations and logits at the fine-tune stage.

4.4   Results on CLUE

As shown in Table 3, it could be found that when the number of parameters drops, the performances of RoBERTa-3 and RoBERTa-6 drop sharply. With the same number of parameters, RBT3 and PKDBERT-3 outperform RoBERTa-3, indicating that both pretraining and fine-tuning distillation are beneficial. Light-BERT achieves the best average score, which demonstrates that the proposed

---

[2] https://github.com/ymcui/Chinese-BERT-wwm.

distillation method could improve the performances of small model effectively. Besides, distillation-based method preforms poorly on task CLUEWSC2020, which indicates that distillation method needs sufficient training data to achieve good performance. Compared with the teacher model, LightBERT-6 is 1.7x smaller and achieves competitive performances; LightBERT-3 is 2.7x smaller and achieves 94.5% of performance of the teacher.

Table 3. Performance comparisons of different methods (%). The best results for each group of student models are in-bold. Ratio refers to the compression ratio on the number of model parameters. The architecture of RoBERTa-3, RBT3, PKDBERT-3 and LightBERT-3 is L-3_H-768 and the architecture of RoBERTa-6, PKDBERT-6 and LightBERT-6 is L-6_H-768.

Model	#Params	Ratio	TNEWS	IFLYTEK	CLUEWSC2020	AFQMC	CSL	OCNLI	Avg
RoBERTa-wwm	102M	1.0x	58.70	62.14	82.57	74.49	81.57	76.34	72.63
RoBERTa-3	38M	2.7x	54.37	58.52	63.82	68.88	54.87	65.25	60.95
RBT3	38M	2.7x	55.06	58.69	65.46	71.55	76.80	70.27	66.31
PKDBERT-3	38M	2.7x	54.06	58.33	67.76	68.72	76.56	72.95	66.40
LightBERT-3	38M	2.7x	**56.21**	**61.41**	**69.41**	**73.38**	**77.57**	**73.59**	**68.60**
RoBERTa-6	59M	1.7x	56.11	59.56	67.76	70.27	74.70	70.03	66.41
PKDBERT-6	59M	1.7x	55.73	59.48	77.63	71.71	**80.87**	75.49	70.15
LightBERT-6	59M	1.7x	**57.64**	**61.56**	**77.96**	74.63	80.47	**75.46**	**71.29**

4.5 Effects of Teacher Assistants

In this section, we investigate the effect of the teacher assistant, which is expected to bridge the gap between the teacher and the student. As shown in the Fig. 3, the introduction of the teacher assistant makes the student model converge faster. Besides, the student model with two teacher assistants converges faster than that with one teacher assistant.

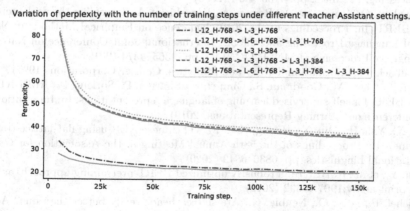

Fig. 3. Variation of perplexity on the validation set at the pre-training distillation stage under different teacher assistance settings. L-12_H-768->L-6_H-768->L-3_H-768 means that the student (L-3_H-768) learns from the teacher assistant (L-6_H-768), which learns from the teacher (L-12_H-768).

5   Conclusion

This paper propose lightBERT, a distilled BERT Model specially for Chinese Language Processing. To adapt to the characteristics of the Chinese language, we adopt whole word masking strategy during the pre-training distillation stage and introduce one or more teacher assistants to compress the model progressively. Experiments on the CLUE benchmark demonstrate effectiveness of our proposed LightBERT.

Acknowledgement. This work was partially supported by the National Natural Science Foundation of China (61632011, 61876053, 62006062), the Shenzhen Foundational Research Funding (JCYJ20180507183527919), China Postdoctoral Science Foundation (2020M670912), Joint Lab of HITSZ and China Merchants Securities.

References

1. Ba, J.L., Kiros, J.R., Hinton, G.E.: Layer normalization. Stat **1050**, 21 (2016)
2. Cui, Y., et al.: Pre-training with whole word masking for Chinese BERT. arXiv preprint arXiv:1906.08101 (2019)
3. Devlin, J., Chang, M.W., Lee, K., Toutanova, K.: BERT: pre-training of deep bidirectional transformers for language understanding. In: Proceedings of the 2019 Conference of the North American Chapter of the Association for Computational Linguistics: Human Language Technologies, Volume 1 (Long and Short Papers), pp. 4171–4186 (2019)
4. Hinton, G., Dean, J., Vinyals, O.: Distilling the knowledge in a neural network, pp. 1–9, March 2014
5. Hochreiter, S., Schmidhuber, J.: Long short-term memory. Neural Comput. **9**(8), 1735–1780 (1997)
6. Jiao, X., et al.: Tinybert: Distilling BERT for natural language understanding. In: Proceedings of the 2020 Conference on Empirical Methods in Natural Language Processing: Findings, pp. 4163–4174 (2020)
7. Kovaleva, O., Romanov, A., Rogers, A., Rumshisky, A.: Revealing the dark secrets of BERT. In: Proceedings of the 2019 Conference on Empirical Methods in Natural Language Processing and the 9th International Joint Conference on Natural Language Processing (EMNLP-IJCNLP), pp. 4365–4374 (2019)
8. Kullback, S.: Information Theory and Statistics. Courier Corporation (1997)
9. Lan, Z., Chen, M., Goodman, S., Gimpel, K., Sharma, P., Soricut, R.: ALBERT: a lite BERT for self-supervised learning of language representations. In: International Conference on Learning Representations (2019)
10. Li, X., Yan, H., Qiu, X., Huang, X.J.: FLAT: chinese NER using flat-lattice transformer. In: Proceedings of the 58th Annual Meeting of the Association for Computational Linguistics, pp. 6836–6842 (2020)
11. Liu, Y., et al.: RoBERTa: a robustly optimized BERT pretraining approach. arXiv preprint arXiv:1907.11692 (2019)
12. Michel, P., Levy, O., Neubig, G.: Are sixteen heads really better than one? Adv. Neural. Inf. Process. Syst. **32**, 14014–14024 (2019)
13. Mirzadeh, S.I., Farajtabar, M., Li, A., Levine, N., Matsukawa, A., Ghasemzadeh, H.: Improved knowledge distillation via teacher assistant. In: Proceedings of the AAAI Conference on Artificial Intelligence, vol. 34, pp. 5191–5198 (2020)

14. Romero, A., Ballas, N., Kahou, S., Chassang, A., Gatta, C., Bengio, Y.: FitNets: hints for thin deep nets. CoRR abs/1412.6550 (2015)
15. Sanh, V., Debut, L., Chaumond, J., Wolf, T.: DistilBERT, a distilled version of BERT: smaller, faster, cheaper and lighter. arXiv preprint arXiv:1910.01108 (2019)
16. Sun, S., Cheng, Y., Gan, Z., Liu, J.: Patient knowledge distillation for BERT model compression. In: Proceedings of the 2019 Conference on Empirical Methods in Natural Language Processing and the 9th International Joint Conference on Natural Language Processing (EMNLP-IJCNLP), pp. 4323–4332 (2019)
17. Sun, Z., Yu, H., Song, X., Liu, R., Yang, Y., Zhou, D.: MobileBERT: a compact task-agnostic BERT for resource-limited devices. In: Proceedings of the 58th Annual Meeting of the Association for Computational Linguistics, pp. 2158–2170 (2020)
18. Vaswani, A., et al.: Attention is all you need. In: Advances in Neural Information Processing Systems, pp. 5998–6008 (2017)
19. Voita, E., Talbot, D., Moiseev, F., Sennrich, R., Titov, I.: Analyzing multi-head self-attention: specialized heads do the heavy lifting, the rest can be pruned. Association for Computational Linguistics (2019)
20. Wang, Q., Li, B., Xiao, T., Zhu, J., Li, C., Wong, D.F., Chao, L.S.: Learning deep transformer models for machine translation. In: Proceedings of the 57th Annual Meeting of the Association for Computational Linguistics, pp. 1810–1822 (2019)
21. Wu, N., Green, B., Ben, X., O'Banion, S.: Deep transformer models for time series forecasting: the influenza prevalence case. arXiv preprint arXiv:2001.08317 (2020)
22. Xu, L., et al.: CLUE: a Chinese language understanding evaluation benchmark. In: Proceedings of the 28th International Conference on Computational Linguistics, pp. 4762–4772 (2020)

Tool Recognition Based on Computer Vision in Nuclear Power Motor Maintenance Scene

Chenjie Pan and Cheng Cai[✉]

Shanghai DianJi University, Shanghai 200240, China
caic@sdju.edu.cn

Abstract. Based on the frequent occurrence of foreign object events in the current nuclear power motor maintenance scene, a foreign object detection method using computer vision is designed. By collecting the image of maintenance tools and using the method of computer vision to identify the content of the image, the limitations of the current detection algorithm for the identification of maintenance tools are found, and the detection algorithm of slender tools is proposed. Research is carried out from the aspects of data set balance, network depth optimization strategy and anchor group expansion and customization. Balanced data sets reduce the bias of network for slender tools. Network depth optimization is proved to be beneficial to the research of slender tools, and the customized anchor plays a significant role. The customized aspect ratio for slender tools greatly improves the receptive field of anchor box, which is more conducive to the detection of slender tools. Compared with the original algorithm, the detection accuracy of the optimized algorithm is improved by 6.91%.

Keywords: Deep learning · Target detection · Residual network · Slender object · Anchor box

1 Introduction

Due to the special characteristics of nuclear power plant, such as high safety requirements, strict risk management and control, resulting in immeasurable huge losses after accidents, foreign matter control is an indispensable part of the operation of nuclear power plant. Foreign object control is very important for nuclear safety.

At present, the inspection of foreign matters in power plants is mainly supervised by means of institutional constraints and human inspection. It includes anti foreign body hierarchical management strategy [1], perfect training mechanism and foreign body event supervision and inspection as the main anti foreign body countermeasures. For the inspection of personnel equipped safety tools and instruments, the way of personnel self inspection and mutual inspection is adopted to supervise the completeness of tools and instruments. In terms of equipment management and personnel management, most of them still use human service, which wastes a lot of financial and material resources. Moreover, due to the characteristics of manual observation, it is difficult to ensure the error free characteristics of management.

Y. Pan et al. (Eds.): AIMS 2021, LNCS 12987, pp. 68–78, 2022.
https://doi.org/10.1007/978-3-030-96033-9_6

In recent years, as a basic work of computer vision, object detection has made great progress and attracted the attention of various fields. Based on the improved target detection algorithm has been widely studied, such as the detection of dense targets and small targets [2], which further expands the application scenarios of target detection [3], and makes the field of target detection achieve more rapid development.

A multi-label classification method based on deep learning is proposed for the detection of surgical instruments in laparoscopic surgery videos. This method combines two state-of-the-art deep neural networks, and uses ensemble learning as a multi-label classification method to solve the tool detection problem [4]. This paper proposes a laparoscopic surgical instrument detection modulation anchoring network based on fast R-CNN, which not only inherits the advantages of the two-stage method, but also maintains the efficiency and speed equivalent to the latest one-stage method [5]. [6] solve the problem of slipping with electric lock screw tools often used in factory production. [7] constructing a U-Net-based network can achieve effective and reliable extraction of tool wear areas.

In this paper, the use of computer vision to detect foreign bodies, making the maintenance process fine. Computer vision technology is used to detect the tools in and out of the power plant, which ensures the completeness of the tools in and out of the power plant, and increases the safety and reliability of the power plant operation.

1.1 Object of Foreign Object Detection

Foreign matter prevention management is an important part of safety production in nuclear power plant. It plays an important role in the manufacturing process, transportation and hoisting, installation process, commissioning process, operation process and maintenance process of nuclear power plant. Once foreign matter control failure occurs, such as foreign matter in system valve, foreign matter in plate heat exchanger, foreign matter in CCS system flushing [8], it will affect the healthy operation of the equipment, or cause damage to the equipment. The causes of foreign body events are different. Through experience summary and analysis, we can find out the root cause of foreign body events. Among the reasons for the introduction of foreign bodies, human factors: the main reason is the tools left by workers [9] (Table 1).

In order to evaluate and analyze the target detection of the tool, the definition of the tool is introduced. Because the tools are divided into many types and sizes, in order to test whether the performance of computer vision method is effective for tool detection, a variety of different types and sizes of screwdrivers, spanners, pliers and tape measure are selected. They include cross screwdriver, slotted screwdriver, precision slotted screwdriver, hammer, spanner 24 mm, spanner 19 mm, spanner 14 mm, spanner 10 mm, adjustable spanner, pliers, scissors, knife and tape measure. They can reflect the general properties of tools, and are commonly used in the detection of foreign matters in nuclear power plants.

1.2 Preliminary Experiment and Conclusion

Because the conventional data set does not have the reference image for the tool detection of nuclear power motor maintenance, this paper uses the form of self built data set

Table 1. Cause analysis of foreign object

Causes of foreign object introduction	Foreign object composition	Number of incidents	Proportion
Environmental waste	Dust, cement, various cloth materials and crane parts falling off during the lifting process of the workshop	7	12.3
Welding defects	Welding slag and weld bead	9	15.8
Imperfect assembly process	Machining metal chips, sandblasting materials	14	24.6
Temporary materials	Temporary plugging materials, temporary reinforcement/support/protection	1	1.8
Clothing and paint are peeling off	Corrosion products, paint debris	4	7
Equipment parts fall off	Loose and falling off parts in equipment due to poor processing and assembly, such as gasket and fastener	6	10.5
Workers left behind	Tools, grinding wheel, mask gloves, mineral water bottle, jewelery, brush, surplus wire, etc.	**16**	**28.1**

to collect the tool image. The collected data set is used for tool object detection and correlation analysis. The data set contains 13 tool categories, and the number of images is 1352. The data set is sufficient, which can be used as a data support tool for target detection problem modeling and analysis.

1.3 Self-built Tool Data Set

In this experiment, the data of self-built nuclear power motor maintenance tool data set is used as the application scenario to verify the algorithm. The resnet-50 network is used to detect the target category. During the training, the optimal model is determined by adjusting the training times and observing the change of loss value on the training set with the number of iterations. The average accuracy mAP of the total data set and each domain data set is used to evaluate the quality of the model.

Through analysis, the average accuracy of the experiment is 84.4%. Through further analysis, it is found that the detection effect is not the best in the relatively slender tool detection, there will be missed and wrong detection, and the average detection accuracy is only 54.6%. On the normal aspect ratio tool, the detection effect is better, and the average accuracy can reach more than 87%.

1.4 Introduction of Tool Definition

In order to evaluate and analyze the target detection of slender tool, the definition of slender tool is introduced. Because the most prominent feature of slender tools and conventional tools is their large aspect ratio, this paper mainly uses the following definitions to quantify the tool fineness:

$$s = min(w, h)/max(w, h) \tag{1}$$

w and h are the width and height of the tool. In order to facilitate the analysis results, the tool with $s < 1/4.5$ is defined as special slender tool (SS), the tool with $1/4.5 < s < 1/3$ is defined as relatively slender tool (s), and the tool with $s > 1/3$ is defined as ordinary tool (R) (Table 2).

Table 2. Definition of slenderness

$s = min(w, h)/max(w, h)$		
$s < 1/4.5$	$1/4.5 < s < 1/3$	$s > 1/3$
Super slender (SS)	Slender (S)	Routine (R)

2 Target Detection Framework Based on Faster R-CNN

In this paper, based on Faster R-CNN, we further detect the target in the image of slender tool. The core idea is to extract some regions with higher target probability from the image of slender tool to be detected by region proposal strategy, and then detect the target. The Faster R-CNN model for object detection of slender tool image based on region proposal is shown in Fig. 1.

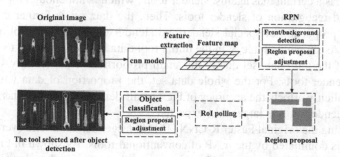

Fig. 1. The frame of Faster R-CNN

Faster R-CNN divides target detection into four modules: candidate region generation, feature extraction, classification and location refinement. Compared with Fast

R-CNN [10], the author unifies four parts into one module, integrating classification information and feature information. The network first extracts the features of the input tool image, then traverses the whole image through the sliding window method in the region proposal network to get the recommendation box and the score of the region, and then inputs it to the ROI pooling layer, through which the feature information of the recommendation box is obtained [11], and finally inputs it to the full connection layer, Get the score of identification classification information and the location information of the area [12].

2.1 Region Proposal Network (RPN)

Region proposal Network (RPN) [13] is a full convolution network, its role is to generate a good region proposal box. RPN and detection network share the convolution feature of the whole graph, which improves the speed of selective search method [14], further shortens the running time of the whole target detection process, and greatly improves the speed of target detection.

2.2 Anchor Boxes

Anchor mechanism is an important part of RPN network. When the size and size of the network detection target can not be determined, it is required to select different size and size boxes to determine the location. This is the important role of anchor. Using anchor point, we can ensure that the conventional tools can enter the detection range of anchor point for different detection targets.

3 Improved Faster R-CNN

3.1 Data Set Optimization

In the process of analysis, it is found that in the tool data set collected at the beginning, the data set has a certain bias against slender tools, which is not enough for good target detection and recognition of slender tools. Then, the data set is further expanded to increase the proportion of special slender and slender tools, and the tool data set* is established. As shown in Table 3, in the initial tool data set, conventional tools account for 80.3% of the total data set due to the small proportion of particularly slender and relatively slender tools. For the whole data set, the proportion of data with different fineness implicitly affects the accuracy of the overall detection, and the bias of the data set against slender tools is larger than expected.

When using the original Faster R-CNN [15] for target detection, the overall mAP of the data set is dominated by the mAP of conventional tools. As shown in Fig. 2, in the tool dataset, all kinds of mAPs are closer to those of conventional tools (r-tools). This bias against slender tools can be mitigated by extending the tool data set*. Through the expansion of the data set, the number of slender tools is increased to four times of that before the expansion, so the bias of tool data set against slender tools is reduced, because the overall mAP is close to that of slender tools. As the proportion of slender tools has

Table 3. Data share of tool data set and tool data set*

Dataset name	Total number of instances	Number of instances		
		Super slender	slender	routine
Tool data set	1352	45	221	1086
		3.3%	16.3%	80.3%
Tool data set*	2453	254	823	1436
		10.4%	33.6%	58.5%

also been relatively improved, the mAP of R tools in tool dataset* is lower than that of the original, but the adjusted dataset has significantly improved the mAP of S and SS tools, and the overall mAP of the dataset has been improved. The proportion of data set is moderate, which is more suitable for analyzing the characteristics of slender tools, so tool data set* is used as the main research object in the following.

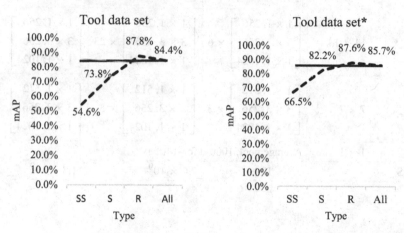

Fig. 2. The mAP of different kinds of objects

3.2 Network Depth Optimization

In the Faster R-CNN network, the selection of convolution network mainly uses RESNET [16] series network for comparative experiments, which are resnet-50, resnet-101 and resnet-152. Resnet-101 thickens the convolution block of the fourth layer on the basis of resnet-50, and resnet-152 thickens the convolution block of the third and fourth layers on the basis of resnet-50. The features that can be represented by shallow neural network are not highly abstract, and the deeper the level is, the higher the abstract degree of features is, that is, the effect is better on some specific tasks [17]. The deeper network can collect more features, including more semantic features. At the same time, when inputting high-resolution images, more implicit semantics can be learned through training [18], such as the information of the screwdriver's Beatles, the size of the wrench, etc., which can achieve better detection results in the deeper network (Table 4).

Table 4. Network structure of ResNet-50, 101, 152

Layer name	Output size	50-layer	101-layer	152-layer
conv1	112×112	7×7, 64, strude2		
conv2_x	56×56	3×3 max pool, strude2		
		$\begin{bmatrix} 1 \times 1, 64 \\ 3 \times 3, 64 \\ 1 \times 1, 256 \end{bmatrix} \times 3$	$\begin{bmatrix} 1 \times 1, 64 \\ 3 \times 3, 64 \\ 1 \times 1, 256 \end{bmatrix} \times 3$	$\begin{bmatrix} 1 \times 1, 64 \\ 3 \times 3, 64 \\ 1 \times 1, 256 \end{bmatrix} \times 3$
conv3_x	28×28	$\begin{bmatrix} 1 \times 1, 128 \\ 3 \times 3, 128 \\ 1 \times 1, 512 \end{bmatrix} \times 4$	$\begin{bmatrix} 1 \times 1, 128 \\ 3 \times 3, 128 \\ 1 \times 1, 512 \end{bmatrix} \times 4$	$\begin{bmatrix} 1 \times 1, 128 \\ 3 \times 3, 128 \\ 1 \times 1, 512 \end{bmatrix} \times 8$
conv4_x	14×14	$\begin{bmatrix} 1 \times 1, 256 \\ 3 \times 3, 256 \\ 1 \times 1, 1024 \end{bmatrix} \times 6$	$\begin{bmatrix} 1 \times 1, 256 \\ 3 \times 3, 256 \\ 1 \times 1, 1024 \end{bmatrix} \times 23$	$\begin{bmatrix} 1 \times 1, 256 \\ 3 \times 3, 256 \\ 1 \times 1, 1024 \end{bmatrix} \times 36$
conv5_x	7×7	$\begin{bmatrix} 1 \times 1, 512 \\ 3 \times 3, 256 \\ 1 \times 1, 1024 \end{bmatrix} \times 3$	$\begin{bmatrix} 1 \times 1, 512 \\ 3 \times 3, 256 \\ 1 \times 1, 1024 \end{bmatrix} \times 3$	$\begin{bmatrix} 1 \times 1, 512 \\ 3 \times 3, 256 \\ 1 \times 1, 1024 \end{bmatrix} \times 3$
	1×1	Average pool, 1000-d fc, softmax		
FLOPS		3.8×10^9	7.6×10^9	11.3×10^9

3.3 Anchor Optimization

Faster R-CNN network uses three sizes and aspect ratio, a total of nine candidate boxes to extract foreground, but these nine sizes are mainly designed for VOC [19], coco [20] and other data sets, which are not suitable for tools such as data containing a large number of slender objects. In this paper, anchor box is redesigned and verified, In order to obtain a more suitable receptive field for slender tools, so as to reduce the number of regression and improve the accuracy and speed of target detection (Fig. 3).

According to the fineness statistics of the tool, the length width ratio of the anchor is set to five kinds, which are 1:1, 1:3, 1:4.5, 3:1, 4.5:1, and the anchor scale is set to five kinds, which are 32 * 32, 64 * 64128 * 128256 * 256. A total of 20 anchor sizes are formed, which improves the accuracy and speed of tool detection. Experiments show that the customized anchor is more conducive to the detection of tool data (Table 5).

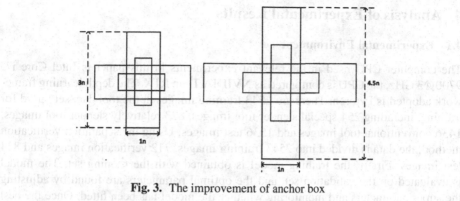

Fig. 3. The improvement of anchor box

Table 5. Improved Anchors size

Anchor size	Anchor proportion
32×32	1:1
32×32	1:3
32×32	3:1
32×32	1:4.5
32×32	4.5:1
64×64	1:1
64×64	1:3
64×64	3:1
64×64	1:4.5
64×64	4.5:1
128×128	1:1
128×128	1:3
128×128	3:1
128×128	1:4.5
128×128	4.5:1
256×256	1:1
256×256	1:3
256×256	3:1
256×256	1:4.5
256×256	4.5:1

4   Analysis of Experimental Results

4.1   Experimental Environment

The computer CPU used in the relevant experiments in this paper is Intel Core i7-9700@3 GHz, the GPU is configured as NVIDIA Titan RTX. The depth learning framework adopted is Pytorch. There are 2543 training images in the tool data set* used for training, including 254 special slender tool images, 823 relatively slender tool images, 1436 conventional tool images and 1536 test images. Using the separation verification method, the data is divided into 2543 training images, 712 verification images and 824 test images. Firstly, the training model is obtained with the training set, The model is evaluated on the validation set, and the optimal parameters are found by adjusting the super parameters and monitoring whether the model has been fitted. Once the best parameters are found, they are tested on the test set for the last time, and the error on the test set is used as the final generalization performance of the evaluation model.

4.2   Experimental Conclusion

In this paper, three kinds of optimization schemes are used to compare the inspection performance of maintenance tools in parallel. When using the data set optimization strategy, networks with different depths can extract deeper information and achieve better detection accuracy than those without optimization. At the same time, the balanced data set reduces the network's bias against slender tools. Because the proportion of slender tools is also increasing, the overall accuracy is improving. After using dataset balance, the overall accuracy for slender targets is improved by 1.6%. The network depth optimization strategy deepens the depth of the network and makes the network get deeper information, such as the difference of screwdriver head, the size of wrench and so on. The detection of slender tools improves the performance. It can be seen that the deepening of depth is more conducive to the detection of slender tools. The conversion from the shallowest network to the deepest ResNet-152 network increased by 3.9%. The effect of anchor point customization is of great significance. The 1:4.5 aspect ratio customized for slender tools greatly improves the receptive field of anchor box, which is more conducive to the detection of slender tools. The method after enriching the size improves the accuracy by 2.2% (Fig. 4 and Table 6).

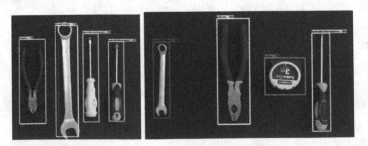

Fig. 4. Detection result

Table 6. The comparison of improved model accuracy

No	Method selection	mAP/%
1	YOLO v2	64.21
2	Faster R-CNN+ResNet-50	84.41
3	Faster R-CNN+ResNet-101	86.58
4	Faster R-CNN+ResNet-152	88.36
5	Faster R-CNN+ResNet-152+Dataset	89.94
6	Faster R-CNN+ResNet-152+Dataset+Anchor	91.32

The experiment also found that when the three strategies are used at the same time, the improvement effect can be superimposed, which further verified that the three methods are good strategies to improve the detection accuracy of slender tools to a certain extent. Faster R-CNN combined with RESNET strategy can effectively solve the problem of neural network degradation, and further improve the effectiveness of the model.

5 Conclusion

This paper mainly focuses on three aspects of tool detection in the scene of nuclear power motor maintenance: 1) define the slender tool in the traditional target detection field, and verify the huge impact of data set imbalance on the slender tool. In the unbalanced state, the bias of network on the slender tool is far greater than that of conventional tools; 2) Using resnet-50, resnet-101 and resnet-152 networks, it is verified that the network depth optimization can improve the detection performance of the network for slender tools, and improve the detection accuracy of the network for slender tools without losing time; 3) By using the anchor mechanism of Faster R-CNN, the abundant anchor styles are expanded, which makes the receptive field of the network more conducive to match the size of slender tools, reduces the number of regression, and enhances the detection performance of the network. The optimized network can improve the detection accuracy of slender tools by 6.91%.

References

1. Zhang, J., Zhang, D.: Exploration on innovative ideas of foreign body prevention management in nuclear power plant. Enterp. Manag. **S1**, 116–117 (2019)
2. Long, J., Shelhamer, E., Darrell, T.: Fully convolutional networks for semantic segmentation. IEEE Trans. Pattern Anal. Mach. Intell. **39**(4), 640–651 (2015)
3. Guo, C., Fan, B., Zhang, Q., et al.: AugFPN: improving multi-scale feature learning for object detection. In: 2020 IEEE/CVF Conference on Computer Vision and Pattern Recognition (CVPR). IEEE (2020)
4. Wang, S., Raju, A., Huang, J.: Deep learning based multi-label classification for surgical tool presence detection in laparoscopic videos. In: IEEE International Symposium on Biomedical Imaging, pp. 620–623. IEEE (2017)

5. Zhang, B., Wang, S., Dong, L., et al.: Surgical tools detection based on modulated anchoring network in laparoscopic videos. IEEE Access **PP**(99), 1 (2020)
6. Yin, X., Zhang, N., Liang, L., et al.: Electric lock screw tool sliding wire detection system and method based on motor characteristics. In: 2020 5th International Conference on Mechanical, Control and Computer Engineering (ICMCCE), pp. 506–509 (2020)
7. Miao, H., Zhao, Z., Sun, C., et al.: A U-Net-based approach for tool wear area detection and identification. IEEE Trans. Instrum. Measur. **PP**(99), 1 (2020)
8. Ren, S., He, K., Girshick, R., et al.: Faster R-CNN: towards real-time object detection with region proposal networks. IEEE Trans. Pattern Anal. Mach. Intell. **39**(6), 1137–1149 (2017)
9. Girshick, R.: Fast R-CNN. Computer Science (2015)
10. Lo, S., Li, H., Wang, Y., et al.: A multiple circular path convolution neural network system for detection of mammographic masses. IEEE Trans. Med. Imaging **21**(2), 150–158 (2002)
11. Kong, T., Yao, A., Chen, Y., et al.: HyperNet: towards accurate region proposal generation and joint object detection. In: 2016 IEEE Conference on Computer Vision and Pattern Recognition (CVPR) (2016)
12. Felzenszwalb, P.F., Huttenlocher, D.P.: Efficient graph-based image segmentation. Int. J. Comput. Vis. **59**(2), 167–181 (2004)
13. Chen, Z., Ye, X., et al.: Small scale pedestrian detection based on improved Fast R-CNN. Comput. Eng. **46**(09), 226–232+241 (2020)
14. Chen, Y., Zhang, S.: Digital image scrambling degree evaluation method based on cross entropy. J. Image Graph. **06**, 997–1001 (2020)
15. Girshick, R., Donahue, J., Darrell, T., et al.: Rich Feature Hierarchies for Accurate Object Detection and Semantic Segmentation (2013)
16. Neubeck, A., Gool, L.: Efficient non-maximum suppression. In: International Conference on Pattern Recognition. IEEE Computer Society (2006)
17. He, K., Zhang, X., Ren, S., et al.: Deep residual learning for image recognition. In: 2016 IEEE Conference on Computer Vision and Pattern Recognition (CVPR) (2016)
18. Gu, Y., Xu, Y.: Structure design of deep convolution neural network for SAR Target Recognition. J. Image Graph. **23**(06), 928–936 (2018)
19. Everingham, M., et al.: The 2005 pascal visual object classes challenge. In: Quiñonero-Candela, J., Dagan, I., Magnini, B., d'Alché-Buc, F. (eds.) MLCW 2005. LNCS (LNAI), vol. 3944, pp. 117–176. Springer, Heidelberg (2006). https://doi.org/10.1007/11736790_8
20. Zhang, K., Zhang, L., Liu, Q., Zhang, D., Yang, M.-H.: Fast visual tracking via dense spatio-temporal context learning. In: Fleet, D., Pajdla, T., Schiele, B., Tuytelaars, T. (eds.) Computer Vision – ECCV 2014, pp. 127–141. Springer, Cham (2014). https://doi.org/10.1007/978-3-319-10602-1_9

Manipulator Posture Estimation Method Based on Multi-eye Vision and Key Point Detection

Aqing Wang and Cheng Cai[✉]

Shanghai Dianji University, Shanghai 201306, China
caic@sdju.edu.cn

Abstract. Image recognition is combined with multi-eye stereo vision technology to estimate the pose of the robot arm which can improve the flexibility of the robot arm control and reduce the immobilization of the control mode. Multiple cameras illuminate the robotic arm to form a multi-eye vision model. At the same time, the HRNet key point detection model detects the key points of the robotic arm in the picture, establishes a space line equation set, and obtains the coordinates of the key points of the robotic arm in space, so as to realize the pose estimation. The experimental results show that when the key points of the HRNet model are detected correctly, the pose of the robotic arm can be estimated well. The method has research significance and practical value.

Keywords: Manipulator · Pose estimation · Multi-eye vision · HRNet

1 Introduction

The robot has the characteristics of high reliability and high precision [1], and has been widely used in various tasks, such as housekeeping service robots, agricultural picking robots, electric inspection robots, express sorting robots, etc. These tasks are accompanied by accurate manipulation of the positions of the joint points of the robotic arm in space. Grasping is a very basic and important skill for robots. Generating a grasping posture for any object has always been a big challenge in the field of robotics [2]. Nowadays, with the rapid development of artificial intelligence technology, image recognition has made great progress, and more and more artificial intelligence is employed to adapt to the changing production environment. As the work becomes more complex, the flexible control of the robot arm is particularly important. In the past, the control of the robot arm in a fixed mode was rather difficult to adapt to the current production mode, so it is necessary to determine the posture of the robot arm more flexibly. This paper uses the posture detection algorithm in image recognition and multi-eye stereo vision technology to estimate the posture of the robotic arm in space.

At present, the mainstream attitude towards detection algorithms includes single-target estimation and multi-target estimation. The single-target estimation networks have

This work was supported by the National Natural Science Foundation of China under grants 62076160 and Natural Science Foundation of Shanghai, China under grants 21ZR1424700.

Y. Pan et al. (Eds.): AIMS 2021, LNCS 12987, pp. 79–88, 2022.
https://doi.org/10.1007/978-3-030-96033-9_7

Convolutional Pose Machines [3], Stacked Hourglass Networks [4], Generative Adversarial Nets [5], HRNet [6]. Multi-target estimation includes top-down and bottom-up modes. The top-down detection mode, first detects the bounding box of the target in the image to reduce the estimation range, and then estimates the pose within the bounding box. The classic algorithms include Faster R-CNN [7], Mask R-CNN [8] and Alphapose [9]. The bottom-up detection mode first detects all the parts of all possible targets globally, and then combines them according to certain rules to get the pose of the target. Related algorithms include Openpose [10], Deepcut [11], etc.

2   System Framework

Multiple cameras are used to form a multi-eye vision scene, and different cameras illuminate the robotic arm from different directions in the scene, and the robotic arm can be fully displayed in the view of each camera. The system gets the pictures of different states of the robot arm from each camera, then calls the trained HRNet key point detection model to detect the key points of the robot arm in the picture. Finally, the key points of the manipulator are calculated by using the method of multi-eye vision space object location, and the pose estimation of the manipulator in space is realized. The system framework is shown in Fig. 1.

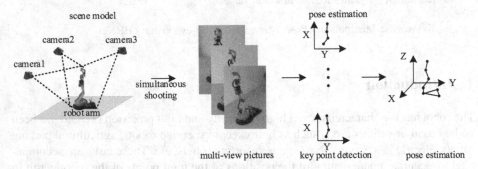

Fig. 1. Pose estimation framework of robot arm in space.

The experiment mainly includes two parts. One is the detection of the key points of the robotic arm. In this paper, the key point detection model HRNet is used to detect the key points of the robotic arm pictures from the camera. The second is that the pixel coordinates of the key points of the robotic arm detected by HRNet in the picture are used as the input of multi-eye vision, and the space linear equations about the key points are established, and the least square method is used to find the optimal solution of the key point coordinates in space.

3   Related Work

3.1   Introduction to HRNet

Ke Sun et al. proposed the HRNet network in order to maintain high-resolution features during the entire pose estimation process. The architecture of the HRNet network is different from the previous pose estimation methods. The previous two-dimensional pose detection network structures mostly sample the high-resolution feature map down to low-resolution, and then restore it from the low-resolution feature map to high-resolution, so as to achieve a multi-scale feature extraction process.

The first stage of HRNet is a high-resolution subnet, and the subsequent stage consists of high-resolution to low-resolution subnets, and then multi-resolution subnets are connected in parallel. HRNet repeatedly exchanges information on multi-resolution subnets to perform multi-scale repeated fusion, and finally outputs high-resolution features for key point estimation. The HRNet network is shown in Fig. 2.

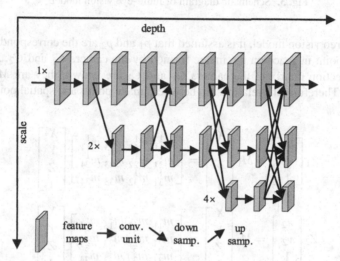

Fig. 2. HRNet network model [6].

Unlike most posture estimation networks, HRNet uses parallel connections to connect high-resolution and low-resolution subnets instead of serial connections. This is why HRNet can maintain high-resolution instead of recovering the resolution from a low-to-high process, and it will be more accurate in prediction. Most existing fusion methods simply merge low-level and high-level features. However, HRNet uses repeated multi-scale feature fusion methods, using the same depth and similar level lower resolution representations to improve high-resolution representations, which will make the high-resolution features more sufficient for pose estimation, and effectively improve the accuracy of predicting heat maps.

3.2 Stereoscopic Spatial Mapping

The pose estimation of manipulator in space needs to use the technology of multi-eye vision. Multiple cameras are fixed in the test environment, and each camera illuminates the robotic arm from different directions. The stereo vision model is shown in Fig. 3.

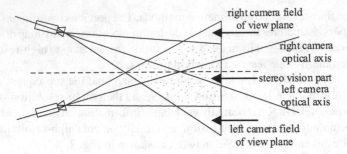

right camera field
of view plane

right camera
optical axis

stereo vision part
left camera
optical axis

left camera field
of view plane

Fig. 3. Schematic diagram of multi-eye vision model.

In the stereo vision model, it is assumed that p_1 and p_2 are the corresponding points of a certain point in space on the image formed by the camera C_1 and C_2. Assuming that the projection matrix of the camera C_1 and C_2 are known, they are M_1 and M_2 respectively. Therefore, the relationship between image points and spatial points can be known.

$$Z_1 \begin{bmatrix} u_1 \\ v_1 \\ 1 \end{bmatrix} = M_1 \begin{bmatrix} X \\ Y \\ Z \\ 1 \end{bmatrix} = \begin{bmatrix} m^1_{11} & m^1_{12} & m^1_{13} & m^1_{14} \\ m^1_{21} & m^1_{22} & m^1_{23} & m^1_{24} \\ m^1_{31} & m^1_{32} & m^1_{33} & m^1_{34} \end{bmatrix} \begin{bmatrix} X \\ Y \\ Z \\ 1 \end{bmatrix} \tag{1}$$

$$Z_2 \begin{bmatrix} u_2 \\ v_2 \\ 1 \end{bmatrix} = M_2 \begin{bmatrix} X \\ Y \\ Z \\ 1 \end{bmatrix} = \begin{bmatrix} m^2_{11} & m^2_{12} & m^2_{13} & m^2_{14} \\ m^2_{21} & m^2_{22} & m^2_{23} & m^2_{24} \\ m^2_{31} & m^2_{32} & m^2_{33} & m^2_{34} \end{bmatrix} \begin{bmatrix} X \\ Y \\ Z \\ 1 \end{bmatrix} \tag{2}$$

Where $(u_1, v_1, 1)^T$ and $(u_2, v_2, 1)^T$ are the homogeneous coordinates p_1 and p_2 in the left and right camera image coordinate systems respectively; $(X, Y, Z, 1)^T$ are the homogeneous coordinates of the space point p in the world coordinate system; m^k_{ij} ($k = 1, 2; i = 1, 2, 3; j = 1, 2, 3, 4$) are the M_k elements in the i-th row and j-th column, respectively. Combining the above formulas, we get the following form.

$$\begin{cases} (u_1 m^1_{31} - m^1_{11})X + (u_1 m^1_{32} - m^1_{12})Y + (u_1 m^1_{33} - m^1_{13})Z = m^1_{14} - u_1 m^1_{34} \\ (v_1 m^1_{31} - m^1_{21})X + (v_1 m^1_{32} - m^1_{22})Y + (v_1 m^1_{33} - m^1_{23})Z = m^1_{24} - v_1 m^1_{34} \end{cases}$$
$$\begin{cases} (u_2 m^2_{31} - m^2_{11})X + (u_2 m^2_{32} - m^2_{12})Y + (u_2 m^2_{33} - m^2_{13})Z = m^2_{14} - u_2 m^2_{34} \\ (v_2 m^2_{31} - m^2_{21})X + (v_2 m^2_{32} - m^2_{22})Y + (v_2 m^2_{33} - m^2_{23})Z = m^2_{24} - v_2 m^2_{34} \end{cases} \tag{3}$$

The geometric meaning of the above formula is the straight line passing the camera C_1 and p_1, camera C_2 and p_2. The spatial point p is the intersection of the above two straight lines, so the above two equations must be satisfied. Therefore, the coordinates of point p can be obtained by combining the above two equations. However, the actual situation will produce a variety of errors, the least square method is usually used to find the best approximate solution of p. The conversion from the spatial point p to the imaging point on the camera view is actually a mapping relationship. The projection matrix of the camera from the spatial coordinates to the two-dimensional coordinates of the image pixels is required, and the formula can be written as formula 4.

$$
Z_c \begin{bmatrix} u_i \\ v_i \\ 1 \end{bmatrix} = M \begin{bmatrix} X_{wi} \\ Y_{wi} \\ Z_{wi} \\ 1 \end{bmatrix} = \begin{bmatrix} m_{11} & m_{12} & m_{13} & m_{14} \\ m_{21} & m_{22} & m_{23} & m_{24} \\ m_{31} & m_{32} & m_{33} & m_{34} \end{bmatrix} \begin{bmatrix} X_{wi} \\ Y_{wi} \\ Z_{wi} \\ 1 \end{bmatrix} \tag{4}
$$

Where $(X_{wi}, Y_{wi}, Z_{wi})^T$ is the coordinate of the i point in space; $(u_i, v_i)^T$ is the imaging coordinate of the i point in the camera view; m_{ij} is the element of the i-th row and the j-th column of the projection matrix to be obtained. Three sets of equations can be obtained from the above formula.

$$
\begin{cases} Z_c u_i = m_{11}X_{wi} + m_{12}Y_{wi} + m_{13}Z_{wi} + m_{14} \\ Z_c v_i = m_{21}X_{wi} + m_{22}Y_{wi} + m_{23}Z_{wi} + m_{24} \\ Z_c = m_{31}X_{wi} + m_{32}Y_{wi} + m_{33}Z_{wi} + m_{34} \end{cases} \tag{5}
$$

Eliminate Z_c in the above equation to get two linear equations about m_{ij}. It can be seen that if n points are known in three-dimensional space, their spatial coordinates are known as $(X_{wi}, Y_{wi}, Z_{wi})^T$, and the coordinates $(u_i, v_i)^T (i = 1, \cdots, n)$ in the camera image are also known, then a total of $2n$ linear equations about each element of the projection matrix M can be obtained, as shown in formula 6

$$
\begin{cases} X_{wi}m_{11} + Y_{wi}m_{12} + Z_{wi}m_{13} + m_{14} - u_iX_{wi}m_{31} - u_iY_{wi}m_{32} - u_iZ_{wi}m_{33} = u_im_{34} \\ X_{wi}m_{21} + Y_{wi}m_{22} + Z_{wi}m_{23} + m_{24} - v_iX_{wi}m_{31} - v_iY_{wi}m_{32} - v_iZ_{wi}m_{33} = v_im_{34} \end{cases}
$$
$$\tag{6}$$

It can be seen from the above formula that the projection matrix M multiplied by any non-zero constant does not affect the relationship between $(X_{wi}, Y_{wi}, Z_{wi})^T$ and $(u_i, v_i)^T$. Therefore, we can make $2n$ linear equations about M, which contains 11 unknown elements. Simplify formula 6 into formula 7.

$$
Gm = H \tag{7}
$$

Among them, G is the $2n \times 11$ matrix on the left side of the formula; H is the 2n-dimensional vector on the right side of the formula; G and H are known vectors. If $2n \geq 12$, it can be solved by the least square method:

$$
m = (G^T G)^{-1} G^T H \tag{8}
$$

Generally, more space points and image point pairs are used to make the number of equations far exceed the number of the unknowns, so as to reduce the error caused by the least square method.

4   Robotic Arm Key Point Detection

4.1   Data Set Introduction and Model Training

This article uses a CMOS camera with a resolution of 1920 × 1080 pixels, and the pixel size is 1.55 μm × 1.55 μm to shoot the robotic arm. A total of 1412 images are obtained, including 1281 images in the training set and 131 images in the verification set. During the image acquisition process, the robot arm is placed on a plane, and the controller is operated to make the robot arm move and take pictures of it. Combining the action characteristics of the robotic arm, manually select the rotation axis of each degree of freedom on the manipulator as the key point of the manipulator. These key point markers will be used for model training of the key points of the robotic arm. The key points of the four degrees (k1, k2, k3, k4) of the freedom of the robotic arm are marked in Fig. 5(a), but other marked points (b0, b1, b2) are only used for visualization, not participating in training. The labeling uses labelme software, which is commonly used in the field of image recognition, as the labeling tool.

Using Ubuntu 18.04 system, equipped with Corei5-9400F central processing unit, GTX1070, 12 GB memory device to train the key point detection model HRNet, a total of 50 iterations, the loss during the entire training process is shown in Fig. 4.

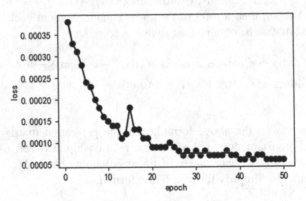

Fig. 4. HRNet model training loss.

It can be seen from Fig. 4 that the model loss after training is 0.00005, which can be used as the key point detection model of the robotic arm.

4.2   HRNet Robotic Arm Key Point Detection Accuracy Analysis

After training on the robotic arm image data set, 118 images of the robotic arm are used to test the trained HRNet model key point detection accuracy. In the process of model testing, the posture of the robotic arm is randomly placed, and there are good and bad detection conditions during the detection process, as shown in Fig. 5 (b).

The box plot is used to draw the key points of the manipulator detected by HRNet model. Suppose the true value coordinates of the key points of the manipulator marked

(a)   (b)

Fig. 5. (a) Marking of key points of the robotic arm. (b) Detection of key points.

by humans are $P_g = (x_g, y_g)$, and the key point coordinates detected by HRNet are $P_d = (x_d, y_d)$, and then the error of the HRNet model detection is:

$$e = \sqrt{(x_g - x_d)^2 + (y_g - y_d)^2} \tag{9}$$

Figure 6 shows the maximum, minimum, mean and some abnormal points of the error between the true value and the detected value of the HRNet model.

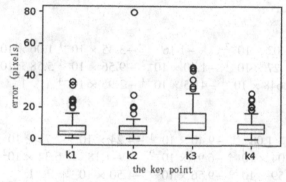

Fig. 6. The distribution of errors between predicted and true values.

Figure 6 shows that the detection error of HRNet for the key points of the robotic arm is around 10 pixels. Due to the shortcomings of the experimental environment and the detection model, there are some cases where the detection is not good.

5 Analysis of Test Results

5.1 Building the Test Environment and Camera Mapping Matrix

In the test environment, three cameras take pictures of the robotic arm at the same time, and the computer receives the picture data from the cameras, as shown in Fig. 7. The image acquisition camera in the experiment is a CMOS camera with a resolution of 1920×1080 pixels and a pixel size of 1.55 μmm $\times$ 1.55 μmm.

In order to obtain the mapping relationship matrix of the camera to the three-dimensional world, the position of the origin of the world coordinate system is artificially

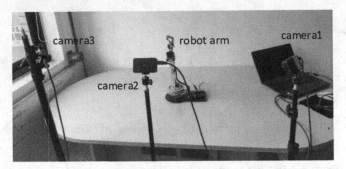

Fig. 7. Experimental scene.

determined, and the directions of the x, y, z axes are set. The coordinate values of n points are measured in the world coordinate system. At the same time, the corresponding image coordinate values of these points in all cameras can be obtained. Suppose the obtained world coordinate is $(X_{r1}, Y_{r1}, Z_{r1})^T \cdots (X_{rn}, Y_{rn}, Z_{rn})^T$, and its image coordinate in the camera is $(u_{r1}, v_{r1})^T \cdots (u_{rn}, v_{rn})^T$, where $n \geq 10$, substituting into the formula 6 to get the projection matrix.

camera1:

$$
\begin{bmatrix}
-6.02 \times 10^{-2} & -1.16 & -3.35 \times 10^{-1} & 1.06 \times 10^3 \\
-1.27 \times 10^{-1} & -1.60 \times 10^{-2} & -9.56 \times 10^{-1} & 5.58 \times 10^2 \\
-6.648 \times 10^{-4} & -4.95 \times 10^{-4} & -2.95 \times 10^{-4} & 1
\end{bmatrix}
$$

camera2:

$$
\begin{bmatrix}
1.08 & -9.40 \times 10^{-1} & -4.24 \times 10^{-1} & 7.71 \times 10^2 \\
2.04 \times 10^{-2} & -6.91 \times 10^{-2} & -1.18 & 6.34 \times 10^2 \\
2.59 \times 10^{-5} & -9.56 \times 10^{-4} & -4.50 \times 10^{-4} & 1
\end{bmatrix}
$$

camera3:

$$
\begin{bmatrix}
1.33 & -1.22 \times 10^{-1} & -6.18 \times 10^{-1} & 7.96 \times 10^2 \\
-1.48 \times 10^{-1} & -2.68 \times 10^{-1} & -1.15 & 7.88 \times 10^2 \\
5.47 \times 10^{-4} & -8.0 \times 10^{-4} & -3.90 \times 10^{-4} & 1
\end{bmatrix}
$$

5.2 Result Analysis

In the experimental scene, the image data of multiple groups of robot arm in different pose are collected, and the key points of the manipulator are detected and calculated, and the coordinates of the key points of the manipulator in space can be obtained. The device parameters used in the experiment are Ubuntu 18.04 operating system, equipped with Corei-9400F processor and GTX1070 graphics card. From the results obtained, the poses of the robotic arm are visually displayed. As shown in Fig. 8, the pose of the robotic arm in space can be better estimated, which is feasible.

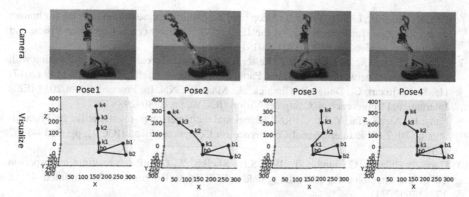

Fig. 8. Visual display of robotic arm detection in different poses.

6 Conclusion

This paper estimates the pose of the robotic arm in space. The HRNet model is used to identify the key points of the robotic arm in the pictures taken by the camera, and the multi-eye stereo vision model is used to establish a linear equation set from spatial points to multiple cameras. Taking into account the actual possible errors, the least square method is used to obtain the optimal solution for the key points. The method detects the key points of the robot arm from the perspective of image recognition. From the perspective of application prospects, the method can fully consider the characteristics of the surrounding environment of the robot arm, without controlling the robot arm in a solidified mode which can improve the flexibility of the robot arm. In future research, we can try other detection algorithms and add more cameras to further improve detection accuracy.

References

1. Farag, R., Saad, M.S., Emara, H., Bahgat, A.: Microscale precision of 6DOF localization rectification of low-end stereo vision using deep learning. In: Proceedings of 2020 IEEE 29th International Symposium on Industrial Electronics (ISIE), pp. 549–554. IEEE (2020)
2. Du, K., Song, J., Wang, X., Li, X., Lin, J.: A multi-object grasping detection based on the improvement of YOLOv3 algorithm. In: Proceedings of 2020 Chinese control and decision conference (CCDC), pp. 1027–1033. IEEE (2020)
3. Wei, S.-E., Ramakrishna, V., Kanade, T., Sheikh, Y.: Convolutional pose machines. In: Proceedings of the IEEE conference on Computer Vision and Pattern Recognition, pp. 4724–4732 (2016)
4. Newell, A., Yang, K., Deng, J.: Stacked hourglass networks for human pose estimation. In: Leibe, B., Matas, J., Sebe, N., Welling, M. (eds.) ECCV 2016. LNCS, vol. 9912, pp. 483–499. Springer, Cham (2016). https://doi.org/10.1007/978-3-319-46484-8_29
5. Chen, Y., Shen, C., Wei, X.-S., Liu, L., Yang, J.: Adversarial PoseNet: a structure-aware convolutional network for human pose estimation. In: Proceedings of the IEEE International Conference on Computer Vision, pp. 1212–1221 (2017)

6. Sun, K., Xiao, B., Liu, D., Wang, J.: Deep high-resolution representation learning for human pose estimation. In: Proceedings of the IEEE/CVF Conference on Computer Vision and Pattern Recognition, pp. 5693–5703 (2019)
7. Ren, S., He, K., Girshick, R., Sun, J.: Faster R-CNN: towards real-time object detection with region proposal networks. IEEE Trans. Pattern Anal. Mach. Intell. **39**(6), 1137–1149 (2017)
8. He, K., Gkioxari, G., Dollár, P., Girshick, R.: Mask R-CNN. In: Proceedings of 2017 IEEE International Conference on Computer Vision (ICCV), pp. 2980–2988 (2017)
9. Fang, H., Xie, S., Tai, Y., Lu, C.: RMPE: regional multi-person pose estimation. In: Proceedings of 2017 IEEE International Conference on Computer Vision (ICCV), pp. 2353–2362 (2017)
10. Cao, Z., Hidalgo, G., Simon, T., Wei, S.E., Sheikh, Y.: OpenPose: realtime multi-person 2D pose estimation using part affinity fields. IEEE Trans. Pattern Anal. Mach. Intell. **43**(1), 172–186 (2021)
11. Pishchulin L., et al.: DeepCut: joint subset partition and labeling for multi person pose estimation. In Proceedings of the IEEE Conference on Computer Vision and Pattern Recognition, pp. 4929–4937 (2016)

3D Pose Estimation of Manipulator Based on Multi View

Xuechun Geng and Cheng Cai(✉)

Shanghai DianJi University, Shanghai 200240, China
caic@sdju.edu.cn

Abstract. 3D pose estimation plays an important role in human-computer cooperation and intelligent control. At present, the manipulator with sensor can realize spatial three-dimensional pose estimation, but the cost is too high. In this paper, the three-dimensional spatial positioning of the manipulator is carried out through the visual label. The two-dimensional pixel coordinates of the visual label on the manipulator are obtained by pasting the visual label on the manipulator and placing three cameras in different directions. By solving the three-dimensional coordinates of the manipulator through the three-dimensional vision fusion proposed in this paper, combined with the least square method to optimize the measurement results, multiple constraint equations can be established through multi-objective vision to improve the measurement accuracy, expand the motion range of the measured object, and have high robustness and economy. In the binocular vision pose detection, 89% of the measurement error within 2 m is less than 10 mm. The detection speed of the robot pose measurement system based on multi vision reaches 16 fps, and more than 96% of the measurement error within 2 m does not exceed 3 mm. Considering the needs of real-time monitoring of industrial detection in the production environment, it needs to have high robustness, and the multi vision pose detection scheme is recommended.

Keywords: Multi-vision · Mechanical arm · Visual label · 3D pose estimation

1 Introduction

At present, the multi-objective vision pose estimation based on visual label [1] has been applied in many fields. Most of the mechanical arms on the market now contain various sensors because of the limited perception of external signals. Radar, laser and vision sensor are commonly used sensors. Traditional pose measurement needs vision sensor to obtain the information of the object to be measured. Its accuracy is mainly affected by the resolution and the distance of the object to be measured [2]. When the resolution is low or the distance of the object to be measured is long, the economy and accuracy of vision sensor will be reduced. In computer vision, the image information of the object can be obtained by placing cameras with different angles and different positions. Based on the multi-objective fusion technology [3], the spatial position and posture estimation is realized. Compared with the visual sensor, the camera has higher economy. The multi-eye vision has better accuracy compared with monocular vision and binocular vision [4].

© Springer Nature Switzerland AG 2022
Y. Pan et al. (Eds.): AIMS 2021, LNCS 12987, pp. 89–98, 2022.
https://doi.org/10.1007/978-3-030-96033-9_8

This paper presents a method of robot arm space pose estimation based on three vision [5]. Based on the visual label detection system, three CMOS cameras are placed in different positions and angles respectively in space to obtain three real-time images of the moving manipulator. The label information includes four corner pixels, center point pixels, and the other is based on the visual label Homography matrix and ID of each tag. The external parameters of the camera are obtained by using the known pixel coordinates and spatial coordinates of the known image by PnP (perspective-n-point) algorithm [6], and the external parameters of the camera can be obtained by the four known points and the internal and external parameters of the calibrated camera, and the origin of the world coordinate system can be determined. According to the label [7] attached to the robot arm, the real-time pixel coordinates of the label can be obtained during the movement of the robot arm. The 3D position and posture in the robot arm space can be reconstructed according to the three-dimensional vision measurement system. The three-dimensional vision measurement system can cover a larger measurement area, and compared with the single binocular vision, the measurement system with three binocular vision has better robustness, and has a wider application in the actual complex application scenarios [8].

2 Position and Pose Measurement System Based on Binocular Vision

2.1 Pose Measurement Model Based on Binocular Vision

The multi eye pose positioning system used in this paper is composed of three cameras equipped with Sony Exmor R COMS sensor, manipulator, visual tag and computer (see Fig. 1).

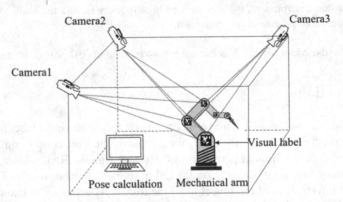

Fig. 1. Three dimensional schematic diagram of position and pose measurement system based on binocular vision.

The system consists of two parts (see Fig. 2), which are camera calibration system and multi camera pose measurement system. The functions of the system include: calibrating the camera to obtain the camera parameters, collecting the data set synchronously, detecting the visual label, transforming the pixel coordinates to the spatial coordinates, and calculating the optimal pose of the multi camera fusion.

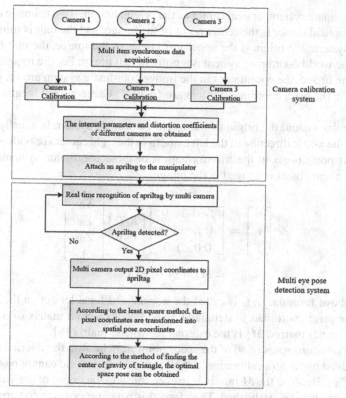

Fig. 2. System flow chart

3 Position and Pose Measurement System Based on Binocular Vision

3.1 Pinhole Camera Model

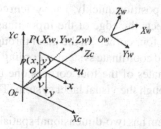

Fig. 3. Pinhole camera model

Image processing involves the following coordinate system: $O_W - X_W Y_W Z_W$: World coordinate system, which describes the position of the camera in m. $O_C - X_C Y_C Z_C$:

Camera coordinate system, optical center as the origin, unit m. $o - xy$: image coordinate system, the optical center is the center point of the image, and the unit is mm. uv: pixel coordinate system, the origin is the upper left corner of the image, the unit is pixel. P: A point in the world coordinate system is a point in real life. p: For the imaging point of point P in the image, the coordinates in the image coordinate system are (x, y), and the coordinates in the pixel coordinate system are (u, v). f: Camera focal length, equal to o and O_C [9].

In binocular vision, the origin of the world coordinate system is usually set at the midpoint of the x-axis direction of the left camera or the right camera or both (see Fig. 3).

The next point is about the transformation of these coordinate systems. In other words, how a real object is imaged in the image.

$$Z_C \begin{bmatrix} u \\ v \\ 1 \end{bmatrix} = \begin{bmatrix} f_x & 0 & u_0 & 0 \\ 0 & f_y & v_0 & 0 \\ 0 & 0 & 1 & 0 \end{bmatrix} \begin{bmatrix} R & T \\ 0 & 1 \end{bmatrix} \begin{bmatrix} X_W \\ Y_W \\ Z_W \\ 1 \end{bmatrix} \tag{1}$$
$$= M_1 M_2 X = MX$$

In the above formula, f_x, f_y is called the normalized focal length on the u-axis and v axis in the pixel coordinate system, and M is $3 \times$ Projection matrix of 3. M_1 is the internal parameter matrix, M_2 is the external parameter matrix [8].

If the pixel coordinates (u, v) of the space point p are known, the internal parameters can be obtained by camera calibration. At this time, the real world cannot be determined (X_W, Y_W, Z_W), Because the M matrix is irreversible and the origin of the world coordinate system needs to be established. Therefore, this paper proposes to construct multiple linear equations by binocular or multi-objective cameras, determine the world origin and get the external parameters of the camera according to PNP, and then estimate the three-dimensional coordinates of the space point P.

3.2 Pinhole Camera Model

The visual label used in this paper is apriltag visual reference system, which can be used in robot, AR, camera calibration and other fields. The system can detect the sign in real time and calculate the relative position quickly. The system consists of the following main parts: the visual detector detects the edge of the input image and the two-dimensional coordinate information of the four corners in the label through gradient detection, establishes the corresponding world coordinate system according to the decoder of the system, and detects the pixel coordinates of the four corners one by one corresponding to the world coordinate system through the visual label system, The monasteric matrix can be obtained.

The visual reference system has two-dimensional spatial information, which is easier to calculate than two-dimensional code. As shown in Fig. 4, the visual label includes multiple categories, and the technology relies on alignment of multiple locating points and auxiliary points. Therefore, the visual reference system can detect a longer distance, and it can also detect in dark or poor detection environment, with high robustness (see Fig. 4).

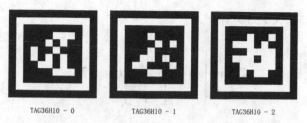

TAG36H10 - 0   TAG36H10 - 1   TAG36H10 - 2

Fig. 4. Some families of apriltag

4 The Model of Three Vision Measurement System

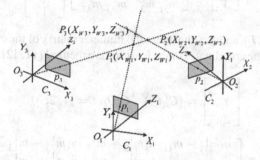

Fig. 5. The model of three vision measurement system

Through the different positions of the three cameras, the image of the visual label on the manipulator is obtained at the same time and in the same scene (see Fig. 5). Through the knowledge of machine vision, a series of two-dimensional coordinates are transformed into three-dimensional coordinates, so as to obtain the pose state of the manipulator [10].

In practical application, because the data is always noisy, as shown in Fig. 5, through the three-dimensional vision fusion, we can get that the three-dimensional coordinates of the measured object are disjoint points P_1, P_2, P_3. After the least square method, the optimal three-dimensional coordinates can be obtained [3]. Let the world coordinate system of P be (X_W, Y_W, Z_W). The optimal objective function should be satisfied.

$$F = \min(P - P_i) \; i = 1, 2, 3 \tag{2}$$

The solution process is as follows:

$$Z_C \begin{bmatrix} u \\ v \\ 1 \end{bmatrix} = \begin{bmatrix} f_x & 0 & u_0 & 0 \\ 0 & f_y & v_0 & 0 \\ 0 & 0 & 1 & 0 \end{bmatrix} \begin{bmatrix} R & T \\ 0 & 1 \end{bmatrix} \begin{bmatrix} X_W \\ Y_W \\ Z_W \\ 1 \end{bmatrix} \tag{3}$$

Among: R: 3×3, T: 3×1:

$$Z_i \begin{bmatrix} u_i \\ v_i \\ 1 \end{bmatrix} = M_i \begin{bmatrix} X_W \\ Y_W \\ Z_W \\ 1 \end{bmatrix} \quad i = 1, 2, 3 \tag{4}$$

The results are as follows:

$$Z_i \begin{bmatrix} u_i \\ v_i \\ 1 \end{bmatrix} = \begin{bmatrix} m_{11}^i & m_{12}^i & m_{13}^i & m_{14}^i \\ m_{21}^i & m_{22}^i & m_{23}^i & m_{24}^i \\ m_{31}^i & m_{32}^i & m_{33}^i & m_{34}^i \end{bmatrix} \begin{bmatrix} X_W \\ Y_W \\ Z_W \\ 1 \end{bmatrix} \tag{5}$$

Where M_i is $A[RT]$, and A is the internal parameter matrix of the camera. According to binocular vision, the coordinates of the least square method [11, 12] can be calculated.

$$\begin{bmatrix} X_W \\ Y_W \\ Z_W \end{bmatrix} = \left(C_i^T C_i \right)^{-1} C_i D_i, \, i = (1, 2, 3) \tag{6}$$

$$C_1 = \begin{bmatrix} u_1 m_{31}^1 - m_{11}^1 & u_1 m_{32}^1 - m_{12}^1 & u_1 m_{33}^1 - m_{13}^1 \\ v_1 m_{31}^1 - m_{13}^1 & v_1 m_{32}^1 - m_{13}^1 & v_1 m_{33}^1 - m_{23}^1 \\ u_2 m_{31}^2 - m_{11}^2 & u_2 m_{32}^2 - m_{12}^2 & u_2 m_{33}^2 - m_{13}^2 \\ v_2 m_{31}^2 - m_{13}^2 & v_2 m_{32}^2 - m_{13}^2 & v_2 m_{33}^2 - m_{23}^2 \end{bmatrix}$$

$$D_1 = \begin{bmatrix} m_{14}^1 - u_1 m_{34}^1 \\ m_{24}^1 - v_1 m_{34}^1 \\ m_{14}^2 - u_2 m_{34}^2 \\ m_{24}^2 - v_2 m_{34}^2 \end{bmatrix} \tag{7}$$

$$C_2 = \begin{bmatrix} u_2 m_{31}^2 - m_{11}^2 & u_2 m_{32}^2 - m_{12}^2 & u_2 m_{33}^2 - m_{13}^2 \\ v_2 m_{31}^2 - m_{21}^2 & v_2 m_{32}^2 - m_{22}^2 & v_2 m_{33}^2 - m_{23}^2 \\ u_3 m_{31}^3 - m_{11}^3 & u_3 m_{32}^3 - m_{12}^3 & u_3 m_{33}^3 - m_{13}^3 \\ v_3 m_{31}^3 - m_{21}^3 & v_3 m_{32}^3 - m_{22}^3 & v_3 m_{33}^3 - m_{23}^3 \end{bmatrix}$$

$$D_2 = \begin{bmatrix} m_{14}^2 - u_2 m_{34}^2 \\ m_{24}^2 - v_2 m_{34}^2 \\ m_{14}^3 - u_3 m_{34}^3 \\ m_{24}^3 - v_3 m_{34}^3 \end{bmatrix} \tag{8}$$

$$C_3 = \begin{bmatrix} u_1 m_{31}^1 - m_{11}^1 & u_1 m_{32}^1 - m_{12}^1 & u_1 m_{33}^1 - m_{13}^1 \\ v_1 m_{31}^1 - m_{21}^1 & v_1 m_{32}^1 - m_{22}^1 & v_1 m_{33}^1 - m_{23}^1 \\ u_3 m_{31}^3 - m_{11}^3 & u_3 m_{32}^3 - m_{12}^3 & u_3 m_{33}^3 - m_{13}^3 \\ v_3 m_{31}^3 - m_{21}^3 & v_3 m_{32}^3 - m_{13}^3 & v_3 m_{33}^3 - m_{23}^3 \end{bmatrix}$$

$$D_3 = \begin{bmatrix} m_{14}^1 - u_1 m_{34}^1 \\ m_{24}^1 - v_1 m_{34}^1 \\ m_{14}^3 - u_3 m_{34}^3 \\ m_{24}^3 - v_3 m_{34}^3 \end{bmatrix} \tag{9}$$

So I got it,

$$
\begin{aligned}
F = \min(\|P - P_1\| + \|P - P_2\| + \|P - P_3\|) \\
= \sum_{i=1}^{3} \{(X_W - X_{Wi})^2 + (Y_W - Y_{Wi})^2 + \\
(Z_W - Z_{Wi})^2\}
\end{aligned}
\tag{10}
$$

To get the optimal objective function, the following conditions should be satisfied at the same time:

$$
f_i = \left\{
\begin{aligned}
(X_W - X_{Wi})^2 + (X_W - X_{Wi})^2 + \\
(X_W - X_{Wi})^2 \\
i = 1, 2, 3
\end{aligned}
\right\}
\tag{11}
$$

According to the method of finding the triangle center of gravity, the optimal 3D pose coordinates can be obtained:

$$
X_W = \frac{1}{3} \sum_{i=1}^{3} X_{Wi}, Y_W = \frac{1}{3} \sum_{i=1}^{3} Y_{Wi}, Z_W = \frac{1}{3} \sum_{i=1}^{3} Z_{Wi}
\tag{12}
$$

In the above formula, X_{Wi}, Y_{Wi}, Z_{Wi} ($i = 1, 2, 3$) is the pose output of three groups of binocular views, X_W, Y_W, Z_W is the pose output of the tricular view.

5 Experiment

5.1 Camera Calibration

Camera calibration [13] is to obtain camera internal parameters, distortion coefficient and other parameters. The common methods of camera calibration include linear calibration, nonlinear calibration, camera self calibration and Zhang Zhengyou calibration method [14]. The experiment adopts Zhang Zhengyou calibration method, and the specific calibration process is shown in Fig. 6. The method is simple and robust. In this experiment, 20 calibration plate images with different angles and positions were collected, and the camera internal parameters were obtained according to the calculated single stress matrix (see Fig. 6).

Fig. 6. Calibration picture

The size of the chessboard used in this experiment is 12×9. By taking pictures of different angles and distances, the internal parameters and distortion coefficients of the camera are obtained according to the calibration software. According to the principle of camera calibration, the internal parameters of the camera are fixed, and will not change because of the change of the pose of the camera, while the external parameters of the camera will change with the change of the pose of the camera. This experiment uses the PNP method to fix the origin of the world coordinate and obtain the external parameters of the camera.

5.2 Experimental Environment Layout

This experiment is based on the movement of the manipulator, through the auxiliary positioning of the visual label to obtain the spatial pose of the manipulator, by drawing the trajectory of the manipulator, measuring the error between the fixed truth point and the estimated point to test the accuracy and robustness of the three eye vision pose measurement system. The physical diagram of the experimental system is shown in Fig. 7.

Fig. 7. Motion picture of manipulator

The pose of the manipulator is acquired synchronously by three cameras. We control the manipulator to swing. The three-dimensional trajectory of the manipulator [15] is shown in Fig. 8 below. The measured values are obtained by measuring different fixed points.

(a)Pose1   (b)Pose2   (c)Pose3   (d)Pose4

Fig. 8. Robot fixed point

The position and attitude measurement system of the manipulator based on the multi vision predicts the motion trajectory of the manipulator (see Fig. 8). The attitude estimation based on the three vision is correct. Because there will be a small amplitude of mechanical vibration in the motion process of the manipulator, there will be slight

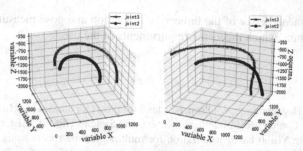

Fig. 9. Fixed point trajectory

frequency in the trajectory drawing. Figure 9 left shows the motion trajectory of joints 2 and 3 under the perspective 1, and Fig. 9 right shows joint 2 under the perspective 2, 3.

During the movement of the manipulator, different positions are taken to measure the measurement values of different joint points. As shown in Fig. 8 (pose1-pose4), the measurement values of different joint points (joint points 1–3) of different positions are obtained. The error analysis of the three eye vision posture measurement system and binocular vision pose measurement system is shown in Table 1 below:

Table 1. Error analysis of binocular and tricular pose measurement

Name	Pose1(joint1)	Pose1(joint2)	Pose1(joint3)
True value	(−55, 40, 180)	(−58, 40, 278)	(−70, 40, 360)
Binocular vision	(−57.6, 43.7, 182.1)	(−62.1, 41.2, 260.9)	(−73.9, 43.9, 365.3)
Tricular vision	(−56.2, 41.1, 179.9)	(−60.3, 39.8, 271.3)	(−72.3, 42.3, 363.7)
Binocular relative error	(4.6%, 9.3%, 1.1%)	(7.0%, 3.0%, 6.2%)	(5.6%, 9.8%, 1.5%)
Three eyes relative error	(2.2%, 1.1%, 0.08%)	(2.4%, 0.4%, 2.4%)	(3.2%, 5.8%, 1.0%)

According to Table 1, it can be concluded that the relative error of x-axis is reduced from 7.0% to 2.4% based on the joint 2 of pose1 of the robot arm measured by three eye vision posture measurement. The relative error of y-axis is reduced from 9.8% to 2.8% for the joint 3 of the robot arm pose1. The relative error of z-axis is reduced from 6.2% to 2.4%, The robot arm 3D pose estimation system can effectively improve the results of binocular vision 3D pose measurement, and has a better accuracy.

6 Conclusion

In this paper, a manipulator spatial pose estimation system based on multi vision is proposed. The manipulator spatial pose can be obtained in real time through a low-cost visual tag system. According to the experimental results, the position and pose estimation of the manipulator based on multi vision can be completed under certain occlusion, which verifies the robustness of the system. Through the experimental error analysis of each axis, the experimental error of the three vision position and pose measurement system is less than 4.9 mm, which meets the requirements of the use.

References

1. Krogius, M., Haggenmiller, A., Olson, E.: Flexible layouts for fiducial tags. In: 2019 IEEE/RSJ International Conference on Intelligent Robots and Systems (IROS). IEEE (2019)
2. Lee, S., et al.: Vision based localization for multiple mobile robots using low-cost vision sensor. In: 2015 IEEE International Conference on Electro/Information Technology (EIT). IEEE (2015)
3. Yu, C., Cai, J., Chen, Q.: Multi-resolution visual fiducial and assistant navigation system for unmanned aerial vehicle landing. Aerosp. Technol. 67(aug.), 249–256 (2017)
4. Peng, J., Xu, W., Yuan, H.: An efficient pose measurement method of a space non-cooperative target based on stereo vision. IEEE Access 5, 22344–22362 (2017)
5. Zarándy, Á., et al.: A real-time multi-camera vision system for UAV collision warning and navigation. J. Real-Time Image Process. 12(4), 709–724 (2014)
6. Zhou, B., Chen, Z., Liu, Q.: An efficient solution to the perspective-n-point problem for camera with unknown focal length. IEEE Access PP(99), 1 (2020)
7. Zhenglong, G., Qiang, F., Quan, Q.: Pose estimation for multicopters based on monocular vision and apriltag. In: 2018 37th Chinese Control Conference (CCC)
8. Wu, L., Zhu, B.: Binocular stereovision camera calibration. In: IEEE International Conference on Mechatronics & Automation, pp. 2638–2642. IEEE (2015)
9. Bračun, D., Sluga, A., et al.: Stereo vision based measuring system for online welding path inspection. J. Mater. Process. Technol. 223, 328–336 (2015)
10. Li, S., Chi, X., Ming, X:. A robust O(n) solution to the perspective-n-point problem. IEEE Trans. Pattern Anal. Mach. Intell. 34(7), 1444–1450 (2012)
11. Xia, R., et al.: Global calibration of multi-cameras with non-overlapping field of views based on photogrammetry and reconfigurable target. Meas. Sci. Technol. 29(6), 065005-1–065005-10 (2018)
12. Shahzad, A., Mu, Y., Gao, X.: Tracking RGB color markers through DLT calibrated monocular vision system. In: IEEE International Conference on Mechatronics & Automation. IEEE (2016)
13. Zhang, J., Zhu, J., Deng, H., et al.: Multi-camera calibration method based on a multi-plane stereo target. Appl. Opt. 58(34), 9353 (2019)
14. Zhang, Z.: A flexible new technique for camera calibration. IEEE Trans. Pattern Anal. Mach. Intell. 22(11), 1330–1334 (2000)
15. Yang, Y., et al.: Multi-camera visual SLAM for off-road navigation. Robot. Auton. Syst. 128, 103505 (2020)

Federated Learning for 6G Edge Intelligence: Concepts, Challenges and Solutions

Han Wang[1,2,4,5]($\boxtimes$), Jianhe Hu[3,4,5], Chunxiao Xing[1,2], and Liang-Jie Zhang[4,5]

[1] Research Institute of Information Technology, Beijing National Research
Center for Information Science and Technology, Tsinghua University,
Beijing 100084, China
[2] Department of Computer Science and Technology, Institute of Internet Industry,
Tsinghua University, Beijing 100084, China
[3] Department of Economics, College of Letters and Science,
University of California Davis, Davis, CA 95616, USA
[4] National Engineering Research Center for Supporting Software of Enterprise
Internet Services, Shenzhen 518057, China
[5] Kingdee Research, Kingdee International Software Group Company Limited,
Shenzhen 518057, China

Abstract. Along with continuous evolution, the future 6G network will become a converged "Cloud-Edge-Terminal" ecosystem which can carry various crucial AI applications on edge computing units, formulating an ubiquitous "Edge Intelligence" paradigm to enable differentiated service innovations and empower intelligent transformation of vertical industries. However, due to issues of data security, user privacy, wireless network transmission capability and etc., it is not feasible for conventional machine learning methods to build AI models by directly collecting massive distributed edge data together, and hence resulting a large number of "isolated data islands" in the edge units. In order to break the data sharing barrier and drive cross-edge data cooperation, this paper studies a federated learning based AI model training method by which sensitive raw data can be maintained and protected in its original edge units. Based on the general scheme, some challenging problems are discussed to implement this new paradigm in practical scenarios, and the corresponding promising solutions and key techniques are proposed to inspire further researches.

Keywords: 6G · Federated learning · Edge intelligence

1 Introduction

Inspired by the idea of cloud computing, the brand new "Service Based Architecture (SBA)" [1] is formulated to support the long-term evolution of the cellular network, from the current 5G to the future 6G and beyond era, so as to meet the critical requirements of various applications. In order to match the whole

This work is supported by National Key R&D Program of China (2018YFB1402701).

Y. Pan et al. (Eds.): AIMS 2021, LNCS 12987, pp. 99–112, 2022.
https://doi.org/10.1007/978-3-030-96033-9_9

new architecture, the Mobile Network Operators (MNO) upgrade their existing telecom equipment rooms into cloud computing data centers, sink the user plane function to the network edges or even user premises, and build the Multi-access Edge Computing (MEC) infrastructures [2–5]. By deploying applications on the MEC hosts, service providers can offer high-quality cloud services with high bandwidth, low latency and massive connections to various kinds of users. In recent years, the rapid development of Artificial Intelligence (AI) technologies, represented by Machine Learning (ML) and Deep Learning (DL), has produced many major breakthroughs in the fields of computer vision, speech recognition and natural language processing, forming a complete ecological chain from smart terminals to cloud platforms and then to application services. By converging technologies of 5G/6G, MEC and AI under the SBA framework, building network edge based ubiquitous intelligence applications will enable differentiated service innovations and empower intelligent transformation of vertical industries. Currently, many cutting-edge 6G researches, represented by the largest international cooperation research project "6G Flagship" [6], have identified "Edge Intelligence" as an important goal in the evolution roadmap from "Cloud Native 5G" to "Intelligence Native 6G" [7–13].

Conventional AI training process is usually concentrated in the cloud computing center, where sufficient and high-quality supply of big data guarantees the quality of model training. However, the paradigm of "5G/6G + MEC + AI" is mainly oriented to vertical industries (e.g. industrial internet, internet of vehicles, and internet of things), where on-premise data in the enterprise's private MEC is exclusive to its owner, and high-value data in the MNO's public MEC cannot simply be opened to the third party due to property rights and security issues as well. In addition, the massive amount of data generated by a large number of smart terminals also cannot be shared due to network transmission capacity and privacy protection. The above restrictions have formed a large number of "isolated data islands" in various edge locations such as MECs and smart terminals, coupled with increasingly stringent data protection regulations worldwide, and hence it has become difficult to complete model training by directly aggregating edge data to the central cloud.

Recently, Federated Learning (FL) is proposed to address the dilemma of "isolated data islands" [14–16]. FL is a distributed ML framework in which each participant does not need to share its raw data in the process of model training, and completes the training procedures jointly by transferring encrypted local model parameters to build a shared global ML model. By using FL to build edge intelligence, the global model can be fully trained under the condition that raw data maintains in its origins. This distributed federated training framework requires only a small number of model parameters to be transferred, instead of aggregating all the raw data from the edge to the central cloud, which can save a lot of network bandwidth and transmission time, as well as save a lot of storage and computing resources in the central cloud, and also fully protect user privacy and data security.

The FL based AI framework is essential to the evolution from "5G Edge Computing" to "6G Edge Intelligence", which will drive cross-field enterprise-level data cooperation, generate new industry and business models based on collaboration, promote innovation development without excessive costs of technology upgrades [17–26]. The paradigm of FL based edge intelligence will enable the 6G system to become an ubiquitous smart information infrastructure that connects everything and empowers industries, supporting the overall development of the entire social economy, and hence has important theoretical significance and practical application value.

This paper discusses some potential challenges and promising solutions to implement federated learning based edge intelligence in the future 6G era. The rest of this paper is organized as follows. Firstly, we introduce the preliminaries of edge computing and federated learning, and propose the paradigm of FL based edge intelligence in Sect. 2. Some potential challenges of conducting the proposed paradigm are discussed in Sect. 3. Then, we propose some promising solutions to defuse the above challenges in Sect. 4. At last, the paper is concluded in Sect. 5.

2 Federated Learning Based Edge Intelligence

Modern communication systems are evolving rapidly, from conventional "terrestrial dumb data transmission channel" to future "space-air-ground-sea integrated smart information grid", during which edge units (e.g., smart terminals and edge computing centers) are playing a more and more important role of producing, caching and processing data. However, most raw data in edge units are so sensitive that they cannot be shared directly resulting isolated data islands. Hence, how to utilize distributed data to construct edge based intelligent applications becomes a tough problem.

Federated learning is one of the most promising techniques to formulate the ubiquitous "Edge Intelligence" paradigm for the future 6G and beyond era. In this section, we introduce the preliminaries of future converged network architecture, discuss the origins of isolated data islands in edge units, and then propose the federated learning based AI model training method.

2.1 Service Based Architecture and Edge Computing

The specifications of SBA [1], defined by the 3rd Generation Partnership Project (3GPP), leverage the service based interactions between different network functions, aligning system operations with network function virtualization and software defined networking to meet the critical requirements in the 5G and beyond era. The similar characteristics above are shared by the MEC specifications [3], which are defined by the European Telecommunications Standards Institute (ETSI). The 3GPP specifications define the enablers for edge computing, allowing that SBA and MEC interact collaboratively in traffic routing and policy control. Integrating the above MEC with SBA, taking the current 5G MEC system for example in Fig. 1, can formulate a powerful edge computing environment providing high-quality cloud services with high bandwidth, low latency and massive connections to various kinds of users.

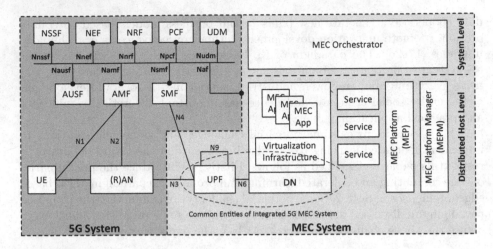

Fig. 1. Typical architecture of MEC integrated SBA (3GPP 5G) system

In the current 5G era, the resources of network and computing are "integrated" together in the paradigm of "5G + MEC". Along with continuous evolution, the future 6G and beyond systems will bring more resources of network, computing and devices together to formulate a "converged" ecosystem, where network resources contain not only high-speed wired fiber links, but also terrestrial and satellite wireless links, while computing resources are ubiquitously distributed in various kinds of clouds, edges and terminals which are abstracted in Fig. 2 and detailed as follows.

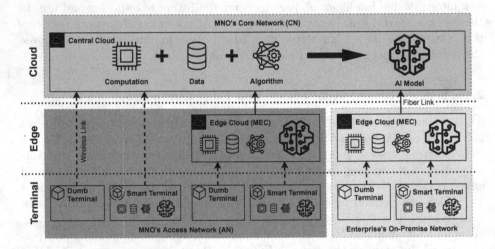

Fig. 2. Computing resources in 6G and beyond systems

- **Cloud** refers to the large scale cloud computing center located in the MNO's Core Network (CN) and connected with edges or terminals via fibers or wireless links, and hence is specifically identified as the "Central Cloud".
- **Edge** refers to a large number of small and medium scale cloud computing centers located at the network edge and providing MEC services, which are widely distributed in the MNO's Access Network (AN) and also can be deployed down to the enterprise premise on demand, and hence is specifically identified as the "Edge Cloud".
- **Terminal** refers to all kinds of user terminal devices, including smart phones, intelligent industrial robots, intelligent connected vehicles and other "Smart Terminals" with rich computing resources, as well as feature phones, cameras, sensors and other "Dumb Terminals" which has only the function of sending and receiving data.

In Fig. 2, the "Central Cloud" and "Edge Cloud" are MNO-managed telecom-grade cloud computing centers with complete and abundant computing resources and high-speed and reliable network connections, which are high-quality platforms for deploying AI services. In recent years, the techniques of smart terminal evolves rapidly so that capabilities of computing, storage and network have increased significantly. Along with the corresponding flourished AI ecology, both of complex inferring and simple training can be achieved on a single smart terminal. As the data producer and privacy concerner, "Smart Terminals" are suitable and necessary to participate the process of training AI models directly. 6G Flagship and other related studies have already regarded "Edge Cloud" and "Smart Terminals" together as "Edge Unit" to host AI applications.

2.2   Isolated Data Islands Dilemma in Edge Units

Building a deep learning based AI system contains two parts: training and inference. The training process requires sufficient data input and intensive computation supply, with the continuous increase of diverse data, and then continuous training is required to improve the model accuracy. On the contrary, the inference process uses the trained model to identify new data in a single step, and hence requires very little computation so that most of the current terminals can achieve such simple inference tasks. Therefore, we mainly focus on the difficult process of AI model training.

The conventional AI training process is usually done centrally in cloud computing centers. The training platform is deployed on the "Central Cloud" in Fig. 2, and all kinds of terminals upload their own raw data directly (or indirectly via "Edge Cloud") to the central cloud, and the central cloud invests a large amount of computation under the control of algorithms to complete the model training process. However, this kind of centralized data aggregation and processing for model training is facing increasing challenges:

- **Transmission**
  The amount of data generated by various terminals is getting larger and

larger, and the continuous uploading of massive multimedia data to the cloud leads to many problems such as high load overheating and frequency reduction of terminals, rapid consumption of battery power, surge in traffic costs and congestion of transmission networks, which seriously affects the normal use of terminals and stable operation of networks.

– **Security**
Along with the rapid development of various vertical industries, the converged system carries more and more enterprise applications, and the massive data accumulated inside various industrial terminals and edge clouds are highly sensitive with many crucial issues such as data property rights, commercial value, personal and enterprise privacy, application system operation security, etc. Moreover, domestic and international data protection regulations are also becoming more and more strict, resulting the raw data can no longer be shared directly.

The above two aspects together lead to a large number of "isolated data islands" at the edge units, which has become a critical dilemma for training large-scale AI models in the converged architecture of the future 6G and beyond era.

2.3   Federated Learning for Distributed Model Training

Federated Learning (FL) is a recent addition to the distributed machine learning approaches, which aims at training AI models across multiple local datasets, contained in decentralized edge units holding local data samples, without aggregating or exchanging their raw data, thus addressing critical issues such as privacy, security and access rights to heterogeneous data. The approach of FL based AI model training is an effective solution to the above mentioned critical dilemma of "isolated data islands" in edge units.

The FL approach is different from both techniques of traditional centralized learning and classical distributed machine learning, where the former requires that all data samples should be uploaded to a centralized cloud server while the latter assumes that all data samples are identically distributed with same dimension. The general FL procedures are designed as iterative steps: training local model with local data samples, and exchanging parameters (e.g., weights in a Deep Neural Network (DNN)) among temporarily trained local models to generate global model. A centralized server can be used as a reference clock to manage the iterative steps of the FL algorithm, while a peer-to-peer scheme without center is also feasible for performing the FL training process.

Specifically, from top to bottom in Fig. 2, "Central Cloud", "Edge Cloud" and "Smart Terminal" are regarded as three-level computing units of which AI training platforms are deployed with the same initial DNN model. Federated learning is performed between the adjacent upper-to-lower (i.e., central cloud ↔ edge clouds, edge cloud ↔ smart terminals, and central cloud ↔ smart terminals) computing units. As illustrated in Fig. 3, the procedures of FL based model training under the framework of Fig. 2 is divided into multiple rounds, each consisting of the following four steps:

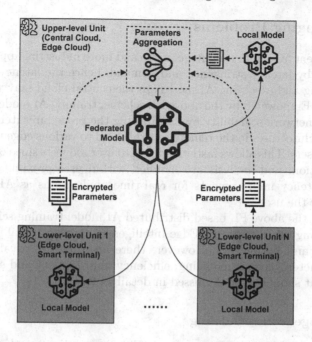

Fig. 3. Procedures of federated learning based model training

- **Local Training**
  All of the computing units calculate gradients or parameters locally, and then the lower-level units forward their trained model parameters to the corresponding upper-level unit.
- **Model Aggregating**
  The upper-level unit performs secure aggregation (e.g., homomorphic encryption) of the uploaded parameters from all lower-level units without learning any local information.
- **Parameter Broadcasting**
  The upper-level unit broadcasts the aggregated parameters to all of the lower-level units.
- **Model Updating**
  All lower-level units update their respective models with the received aggregated parameters, and then examine the performances of updated models.

After several local training and update exchanges between the upper-level unit and the corresponding lower-level units, it is possible to achieve a global optimal learning model. It is worth noting that, according to the source and feature of datasets, "horizontal" or "vertical" federating scheme can be chosen to perform model parameters aggregation to achieve "cross-sample collaborative modeling in the same industry" or "cross-feature collaborative modeling among different industries" to better meet the needs of practical applications.

3   Challenging Problems

From the current 5G era to the future, more and more industrial applications are characterized by latency stringency and demand, hence the latency induced by communicating and executing AI models in the central cloud may violate these requirements. Empowered by the above FL scheme, training AI model at the edge units ensures network scalability by distributing the procedures iteratively from centralized architectures in the remote central cloud to various edge units located closer to the users. This allows faster response to user requests since computation, data aggregation, and analysis are handled within user proximity. Moreover, it provides latency improvements for real-time applications as AI models are executed near the user.

Therefore, the above FL based distributed AI model training scheme is suitable for building the ubiquitous "Edge Intelligence" for the critical requirements of future 6G and beyond era. However, there are some practical challenging problems in heterogeneous modeling, efficiency improvement and security reinforcement that should to be discussed in detail as follows.

3.1   Heterogeneous Modeling

The performances of computing units in Fig. 2 vary significantly, from stable and efficient cloud computing centers to resource-constrained smart terminals, forming a heterogeneous model training system. In the standard FL training process described in Sect. 2.3, the upper-level unit can only aggregate parameters to renew the federated model after receiving all of the lower-level parameters before executing the subsequent steps. However, in a practical system, smart terminals may often fail to upload model parameters in time or even lose connections with their upper-level unit, due to unstable network connection, overheating frequency reduction, battery volume exhaustion, etc., which will result a halt of the whole process of model training. Since there are massive smart terminals participating the process of federated model training, the above halt phenomenon is almost bound to occur unavoidably.

In order to solve the above problems, it is necessary to study the federated modeling method applicable to heterogeneous edge units, so as to reduce the impact of terminal anomalies to ensure smooth and efficient in process of FL based training.

3.2   Efficiency Improvement

Currently, AI techniques are mainly used for processing multimedia contents, such as image recognition or video analysis, which requires high-dimensional DNN models with massive parameters to describe complex multimedia data. Although the FL based distributed training scheme does not require uploading raw multimedia data, the frequent exchanges of massive model parameters between upper and lower levels will also put certain stress on the network transmission capability. Edge cloud is connected to central cloud through high-stable high-speed fiber network, and hence the parameters are transferred smoothly and fluidly. However, smart terminals are usually connected to edge or central cloud through wireless links, which are susceptible to various factors and poor network stability, and hence the frequent exchange of massive parameters may encounter transmission bottlenecks so as to affect the overall training efficiency.

In order to solve the above problems, it is necessary to study the efficient training methods for high-dimensional models, so as to improve the efficiency of model parameter exchange to ensure a high-efficient federated training process.

3.3 Security Reinforcement

As described in Sect. 2.3, the upper-level unit plays an important role in aggregating lower-level parameters and renew the federated model, which is the "critical core" in the framework of federated training. Although the upper-level unit is served by central or edge cloud with complete security measures, such a training system with center may still be subject to security threats from its inside. It has been shown that the original raw data can be deduced out with high probability by tracking gradient changing process during the model training. If the "critical core" is invaded by an attacker, the malicious program can collect all parameters during the entire process of model training, and may recover the original raw data through decryption, deduction and other technical methods, which will pose a great threat to user privacy, business interests, and even system operation security.

In order to solve the above problems, it is necessary to study the decentralized security reinforcement methods and build a safe and reliable federated training mechanism to ensure the operation security of the edge intelligence systems.

4 Promising Solutions

The above mentioned problems involve three aspects of federated modeling, i.e., heterogeneity, efficiency and security, which are practical challenges in the future 6G and beyond era. In order to inspire further researches, we will propose some promising ideas to solve the above challenges, which are inducted as a logical diagram in Fig. 4 and discussed in detail as follows.

4.1 Federated Modeling for Heterogeneous Edge Units

The standard FL training process requires all of the lower-level parameters collected together before aggregating uniformly, which is a "synchronous" strategy of parameter aggregation. However, in the heterogeneous model training system described in Sect. 3.1, due to the limitations of wireless networks and smart terminals, it is not guaranteed that all smart terminals can upload their model parameters in time, and some ones may even be temporarily or permanently disconnected, which will cause the entire training process to stagnate. Therefore, in the practical heterogeneous system, we need to propose an "asynchronous"

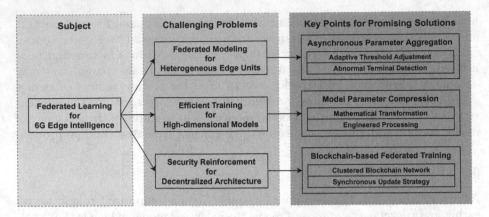

Fig. 4. Promising solutions to federated learning based edge intelligence

parameter aggregating strategy to reduce the impact of terminal and network anomalies to ensure efficient and smooth during the training process.

Specifically, considering the limited capacities of wireless network and terminals, we only require smart terminals to "do their best" to upload parameters. When the number or proportion of received parameters reaches a certain "threshold", the upper-level unit instantly start to perform parameter aggregation to build the federated model. Few terminals, which cannot upload in time and join the current round of parameter aggregation, can participate in the next aggregating round after their parameters have been uploaded completely. It is worth noting that how to determine an appropriate threshold is an important issue. If the threshold is set too low, the parameters will be aggregated so early that the new federated model improves little due to insufficient parameter collection, and hence more training rounds are needed to get a better modeling quality. On the contrary, if the threshold is set too high, the waiting time will be too long to pull down the training efficiency. Therefore, the threshold should be adjusted adaptively and dynamically according to different datasets, models and training stages. Moreover, during multiple rounds of parameter aggregation, if a terminal consistently fails to complete uploading tasks, the upper-level unit should identify it as a suspected abnormal terminal. Once detected and confirmed, it will be removed from the lower-level units list to avoid lowering the proportion of valid units and affecting the model training efficiency.

The above proposed "Asynchronous Parameter Aggregation" strategy can greatly reduce the waiting time of upper-level units and improve the entire efficiency of federated model training. The corresponding key points are summarized in Fig. 4 and explained as follows:

– **Adaptive Threshold Adjustment**
By tracking the real-time convergence state during the process of federated model training, the threshold can be determined adaptively to balance the training speed and accuracy.

- **Abnormal Terminal Detection**
  The management entities (e.g., Access and mobility Management Function (AMF) in Fig. 1) on control plane can be utilized to detect working status of suspected abnormal terminals, which will be removed to avoid low efficiency once be confirmed as anomaly.

The proposed adaptive threshold adjustment algorithm and the abnormal terminal detection method together can formulate an adaptive asynchronous parameter aggregation mechanism to ensure an efficient and smooth process of federated modeling training.

4.2   Efficient Training for High-Dimensional Models

The FL based distributed training requires frequent exchange of model parameters between adjacent upper-to-lower computing units, and hence the communication efficiency between upper and lower levels is crucial to the overall efficiency of federated modeling. Under the condition of constant network transmission capacity, improving the communication efficiency can be considered from a combination of two aspects: on the one hand, reducing the round number of parameter exchange, which is the main issue discussed in the previous section of asynchronous parameter aggregation; on the other hand, reducing the data volume in every exchange to save transmission time, which is the main topic of this section.

High-dimensional DNN models can better describe complex multimedia data, but also bring a huge amount of model parameters which put greater pressure on the processes of homomorphic encryption, wireless transmission and secure aggregation during federated training. However, it has been shown that not every value of the massive parameters in the high-dimensional model plays an important role which has a large amount of redundancy, and additionally the model parameters and the gradient changes in the training process often have certain structural and sparse features, and thus providing basic premises to compress the model parameters and reduce the amount of data.

Specifically, the high-dimensional "Model Parameter Compression" can be achieved by performing two types of methods, "Mathematical Transformation" and "Engineered Processing", which are summarized in Fig. 4 and explained as follows:

- **Mathematical Transformation**
  According to structural and sparse features, some mathematical transformation methods, such as singular value decomposition, Huffman coding, principal component analysis and compressive sensing, can be used to indirectly reduce data volume to compress the high-dimensional model. This kind of methods utilizes the inherent structure and sparsity of the original raw data to compress model parameters, usually with advantages of high compression rate and lossless, but suffering the drawback of computational intense.

- **Engineered Processing**
  Many conventional engineering methods, such as quantification, dimensionality reduction, pruning, truncation and precision reduction, can be used to directly reduce the amount of model parameters, which is simple and efficient to implement, but usually with a defect of lossy compression.

After data processing, the amount of model parameters will be significantly reduced, which can consequently improve the communication efficiency during the federated training process. It is worth noting that most commonly used methods are precision-impaired which may degrade the modeling quality due to the cumulative effects of continuous iterations between upper and lower units, while a few lossless methods are computational complex which may also increase burden on smart terminals. Therefore, it is necessary to choose appropriate compression methods, according to features of actual business data and model structures, balancing computation-communication-storage overheads and modeling accuracy, so as to perform high-dimensional model training more efficiently.

4.3 Security Reinforcement for Decentralized Architecture

In the process of federated training, the upper-level unit plays an important role as the "critical core", which may lead to a serious systematic security risk once be invaded. Therefore, we need to strengthen the system architecture with the idea of "decentralization" to ensure the secure operation of edge intelligence systems.

In recent years, the rapidly developing technology of "Blockchain", with anonymous, immutable and distributed features, has been widely used to provide a reliable secure system among multiple untrustworthy participants. By transforming the conventional centralized network structure to distributed, the blockchain is essentially a distributed ledger which can ensure the data security by various cryptographic techniques and guarantee the data reliability among multiple untrustworthy distributed participants through consensus mechanisms, smart contracts, etc. In the federated training process, the upper and lower units naturally formulate as a distributed architecture, and hence all of the computing units can join together in a blockchain network and share equivalent rights. Each computing unit updates the global record in the whole blockchain network when interacting model parameters, so that each on-chain unit records the whole changing process of model parameters and thus the "critical core" is decentralized from a single upper-level unit to the whole network. Under the constraints of consensus mechanism and smart contracts, illegal operations initiated by malicious nodes at any network location will be discovered in time, and hence the security risks in the federated training process can be fundamentally solved.

It is worth noting that latency will be introduced during the process of updating blockchain. The larger the network scales, the greater the latency introduces, and excessive scale of the blockchain will suffers too large additional delay to operates normally. Therefore, in order to maintain high-efficiency, the "Blockchain-based Federated Training" should be operated as a "Clustered

Blockchain Network" with "Synchronous Update Strategy", of which key points are summarized in Fig. 4 and explained as follows:

- **Clustered Blockchain Network**
  According to the physical and logical architecture of the practical federated training system, various of engineering methods, such as slicing, sub-chaining and multi-channelization, can be utilized to split a large-scale blockchain into clustered sub parts to avoid long-latency and low-efficiency.
- **Synchronous Update Strategy**
  The intra-cluster (i.e., within a particular slice, sub-chain or channel) data are synchronously updated to promote efficiency, while the updating strategy of inter-cluster (i.e., between slices, sub-chains and channel) data maintains asynchronous to avoid big changes of the FL training process.

The above proposed clustered blockchain network structure and its corresponding synchronous update strategy can effectively balance efficiency and security to guarantee stable operation of the blockchain-based federated training system.

5 Conclusion

In this paper, we studied a federated learning based distributed training method, which is dedicated to solving the isolated data islands and breaking the data sharing barrier, to facilitate building ubiquitous edge-based AI applications in the future 6G and beyond era. We first proposed the general scheme of federated training, and then discussed three challenging aspects of heterogeneous modeling, efficiency improvement and security reinforcement in practical scenarios. Based on the discussed problems, we proposed some promising ideas and corresponding key technical points to inspire further researches.

References

1. 3GPP TS 23.501 V16.8.0: Technical Specification Group Services and System Aspects; System architecture for the 5G System (5GS); Stage 2 (Release 16). 3GPP Technical Specification (2021)
2. ETSI MEC: https://www.etsi.org/technologies/multi-access-edge-computing
3. ETSI GS MEC 003 V2.1.1: Multi-access Edge Computing (MEC); Framework and Reference Architecture. ETSI Group Specification (2019)
4. Kekki, S., et al.: MEC in 5G networks. ETSI White Paper, pp. 1–28 (2018)
5. ETSI GR MEC 031 V2.1.1: Multi-access Edge Computing (MEC); MEC 5G Integration. ETSI Group Report (2020)
6. 6G Flagship Homepage. https://www.6gflagship.com/
7. 6G Flagship: Key Drivers and Research Challenges for 6G Ubiquitous Wireless Intelligence. https://www.6gchannel.com/items/key-drivers-and-research-challenges-for-6g-ubiquitous-wireless-intelligence/
8. Peltonen, E., et al.: 6G white paper on edge intelligence. 6G Research Visions (8) (2020). https://www.6gchannel.com/items/6g-white-paper-edge-intelligence/

9. Samsung Research: 6G: The Next Hyper-Connected Experience for All. Samsung Research Report (2020)
10. IMT-2030 (6G) Promotion Group: White Paper on 6G Vision and Candidate Technologies. IMT-2030 (6G) Promotion Group White Paper (2021)
11. 6GANA: From Cloud AI to Network AI: A View from 6GANA. 6GANA Report (2021)
12. NTT DOCOMO: White Paper: 5G Evolution and 6G (Version 3.0). NTT DOCOMO White Paper (2021)
13. 5G PPP: AI and ML - Enablers for Beyond 5G Networks (Version 1.0). 5G PPP White Paper (2021)
14. Konečný, J., McMahan, H.B., Yu, F.X., Richtarik, P., Suresh, A.T., Bacon, D.: Federated learning: strategies for improving communication efficiency. In: NIPS Workshop on Private Multi-Party Machine Learning (2016)
15. McMahan, H.B., Moore, E., Ramage, D., Hampson, S., Arcas, B.A.: Communication-efficient learning of deep networks from decentralized data. In: Proceedings of the 20th International Conference on Artificial Intelligence and Statistics (AISTATS) (2017)
16. Yang, Q., Liu, Y., Chen, T., Tong, Y.: Federated machine learning: concept and applications. ACM Trans. Intell. Syst. Technol. **10**(2), 1–19 (2019)
17. You, X., et al.: Towards 6G wireless communication networks: vision, enabling technologies, and new paradigm shifts. Sci. China Inf. Sci. **64**(1), 110301 (2020). https://doi.org/10.1007/s11432-020-2955-6
18. Wang, X., Han, Y., Wang, C., Zhao, Q., Chen, X., Chen, M.: In-edge AI: intelligentizing mobile edge computing, caching and communication by federated learning. IEEE Netw. **33**(5), 156–165 (2019)
19. Liu, Y., Yuan, X., Xiong, Z., Kang, J., Wang, X., Niyato, D.: Federated learning for 6G communications: challenges, methods, and future directions. China Commun. **17**(9), 105 (2020)
20. Wang, X., Han, Y., Leung, V.C.M., Niyato, D., Yan, X., Chen, X.: Convergence of edge computing and deep learning: a comprehensive survey. IEEE Commun. Surv. Tutor. **22**(2), 869–904 (2020)
21. Niknam, S., Dhillon, H.S., Reed, J.H.: Federated learning for wireless communications: motivation, opportunities, and challenges. IEEE Commun. Mag. **58**(6), 46–51 (2020)
22. Lim, W.Y.B., et al.: Federated learning in mobile edge networks: a comprehensive survey. IEEE Commun. Surv. Tutor. **22**(3), 2031–2063 (2020)
23. Feng, C., Zhao, Z., Wang, Y., Quek, T.Q.S., Peng, M.: On the design of federated learning in the mobile edge computing systems. IEEE Trans. Commun. **69**(9), 5902–5916 (2021)
24. Lu, Y., Huang, X., Zhang, K., Maharjan, S., Zhang, Y.: Blockchain and federated learning for 5G beyond. IEEE Netw. **35**(1), 219–225 (2021)
25. Yu, R., Li, P.: Toward resource-efficient federated learning in mobile edge computing. IEEE Netw. **35**(1), 148–155 (2021)
26. Zhou, X., Liang, W., She, J., Yan, Z., Wang, K.I.K.: Two-layer federated learning with heterogeneous model aggregation for 6G supported internet of vehicles. IEEE Trans. Veh. Technol. **70**(6), 5308–5317 (2021)

Author Index

Printed in the United States
by Baker & Taylor Publisher Services

Printed in the United States
by Baker & Taylor Publisher Services